"Written by thirty-one different men from varying backgrounds, **Under Construction** is a blueprint for becoming the man God intends you to be. Addressing topics relevant to every man's life, this compilation book will inspire you to use the tools given in God's Word and allow the Holy Spirit to do His work of building in your life."
—**Mark Batterson,** *New York Times best-selling author of "The Circle Maker," Lead Pastor of National Community Church*

"There is a renewed focus on developing the man God wants to bless. Ministries are going beyond the men's breakfasts and golf leagues, as good as those are. **Under Construction** is where it gets real! Deconstruction, clearing the landscape of the pitfalls and traps that have crippled too many men and their families, and building a solid foundation of faith and faithfulness is only the beginning.

In **Under Construction,** Jamie Holden and his team take you through the process of building a protective, powerful covering for you and your family so that in the end we all might "Live the Life" Jesus intended us to live. Fulfill your potential! Start clearing the land and building the life you always wanted. **Under Construction** has the blueprints to get you there!"
— **Dr. Duane P Durst,** *Superintendent, New York Ministry Network, Executive Presbyter, General Council of the Assemblies of God*

"Jamie Holden has committed his life and ministry to leading men into a deeper relationship with Jesus Christ! In this culture, men need to see authentic followers of Jesus who reflect, both His character and actions. Jamie Holden is one those! In **Under Construction**, he has gathered a group of men to come together to help men from all walk　　　　　　　c anointing on Mantour Ministries to l　　　　　　　Christ!"
—Shane Wilson, *Lead*

D1473039

"Mantour Ministries has done an amazing job in collaborating seasoned ministers with common topics relevant to building a strong relationship between God and men who desire to follow a biblical model of doing life. Set in the context of a construction project, *Under Construction* moves through themes that take spiritual formation from necessary demolition to a move-in ready rebuild. This book would be a great read for individual devotions or a group study discussion starter. It is filled with pastoral perspective and challenge that emerges from men who have experience working with other men. I recommend this book for men who want to build a solid life and legacy."

—**Donald J. Immel**, *Penn-Del Ministry Network Secretary-Treasurer*

UNDER CONSTRUCTION

M*NTOUR MINISTRIES

4One
Ministries
www.4oneministries.org

UNDER CONSTRUCTION

DEDICATION

This book is dedicated to Jesus, the Master Builder, who is constantly working in all of our lives.

We'd also like to thank Tom Rees for taking a chance on Mantour Ministries five years ago and allowing all of us to grow under construction together.

CONTENTS

SECTION 4: ROOFING: BUILDING A COVERING FOR YOUR FAMILY

SECTION 5: WIRING: CONNECTING TO THE POWER SOURCE

ACKNOWLEDGMENTS

I would like to thank my colleagues, who are also my friends, for their willingness to contribute to and be a part of this project. I appreciate each one of you for your hard work and willingness to serve. I value our friendship and appreciate your heart to see men's ministry grow and thrive.

I would like to thank Lee Rogers and Jason Tourville for consulting with me and advising me on the editing and compiling of this project. I wouldn't have been able to do it without your wisdom and advice.

I would also like to thank all of the wives, personal assistants, children, friends, and associates who helped each author edit their chapters before sending them to us to compile. Your hard work was noticed and greatly appreciated it.

A special thanks to Courtney Di Trolio for all her hard work and effort on proofreading and editing this book. You did a fabulous job!

Finally, I want to thank Adessa Holden for the MANY hours she spent editing this book with me, researching sources, and verifying Scripture references. Your hours of painstaking work are so appreciated, and this book could not have been completed without your hard work and perseverance.

Thank you to all of you!

-Jamie Holden

President/CEO 4One Ministries, Inc.
Founder/Director Mantour Ministries

INTRODUCTION

By Jamie Holden

When I was a young boy, every Saturday night my dad would watch This Old House with Bob Vila. For those of you who aren't familiar with the show, it was the original "fixer-upper show." Long before there were entire cable networks and internet channels devoted to home repair, Bob Vila was the pioneer of home improvement. Every week, my Dad would watch him as Bob took an old, dilapidated building and repaired it into a dream home.

And every weekend I would wonder, "Isn't there anything else on television?"

It was a typical thought for a young boy more interested in play than work. Little did I know that years later when I matured and felt the responsibility of maintaining, repairing and even building onto a house, I'd be the one watching YouTube videos learning the basics of construction. Oh how the years change us!

Of course, the same can be said of our spiritual lives. As we mature as men and realize our God-given responsibility to be godly men in our jobs, our relationships, our churches, and in our communities, we quickly realize we have a lot to learn. Just like a squeaky door, a cracked wall, or a dripping sink, the obstacles and struggles in our lives remind us that, we too, are always under construction. We're all in the process of learning, growing, and changing from what we are into the men that God desires us to be. None of us has arrived… we're all under construction.

In this book, we're going to discuss several of the major areas where we, as men, can learn from each other as the Master Builder continues His construction project in our lives. Call it a spiritual, "how-to" book. Some of the topics we're going to discuss are:

1. Mind Demolition: Blowing Up Your Strongholds

2. Building a Firm Foundation

3. Framing: Building Godly Character

4. Roofing: Building a Covering for Your Family

5. Wiring: Connecting to the Power Source

6. Moving In: Reaching Your Full Potential as a Man of God

Here's the reason I'm really excited about this book---it isn't just written by one man. Instead, each chapter is written by a different man lending his own background and experiences from his journey toward becoming a man of God. Because even though we all have our own stories, as men, we are all struggling with the same areas. Just like Bob Vila gave his tips to wannabe home improvers years ago, we've come together to share our tips for allowing God to work in our lives and reconstruct us into the men He wants us to be.

I'm so happy you've chosen to join us on this journey.

Let's get started Under Construction…..

SECTION 1:

Mind Demolition: Blowing Up Your Strongholds

THE PROBLEM IS UNDER THE HOOD

By Brian Donnachie

Except for the geyser that would squirt up from the gearshift whenever I ran over a puddle, it was a great little car! My part-time job in my junior year of high school made it possible to buy the five-year-old beauty! The 1973 Opel Manta was imported by General Motors and was a sporty little ride! The small coup boasted a blue and black paint job, a tight engine, manual five-speed shift on the floor, and a kicking quadraphonic sound system with AM–FM radio and a cassette tape deck.

What's not to love? I would take my future wife out on a date, put the pedal to the metal, and pray it didn't rain!

Unfortunately, it also had a few engine issues and had to remain parked until my father could get under the hood and fix the problem. One day, I made the mistake of parking it under a mulberry tree in my parents' yard. Because the engine would not start, I was unable to move the Opel from the incessant berry bombs that both the tree and the birds strategically distributed all over the hood, roof, trunk, and windows!

That's when I decided I would get the bucket and soap and give the car a bath. My father walked by me and said, "Son, until that engine is fixed, it will do no good to wash the car! The problem is under the hood!"

Some things you just remember! It may not be particularly profound at the moment when spoken, but years later, things have a way of surfacing.

After dad got under the hood (with very little help from me), the car was fixed. I gave it an amazing wash and wax and would never park under that tree again!

It is intriguing that the Lord Jesus made a similar point in referring to food and the endless Mosaic laws regarding what and how to eat. His point was that it's what's on the inside of a person that is the problem, not the outside.

> *What goes into a man's mouth does not make him 'unclean,' but what comes out of his mouth, that is what makes him 'unclean.' (Matthew 15:11, NIV)*

In other words, it's what's under the hood that determines one's functionality and position, and not the outward actions.

Question: Why is this principle so important?

Answer: Before we can get the "what we do" to get our daily lives in order, it is essential to get under the hood to "what we are" and fix it!

You might want to read that again!

In order to bring about any real power for breaking entrenched patterns of behavior, we must embrace this simple yet profound truth. We have to deal with the root before we can deal with the fruit!

CAN I GET THERE FROM HERE?

Where do you want to go from here?

Do you know?

Where do you really want to go?

Do you want to experience the break in the cycle of addiction and sin?

In his classic work, *Alice's Adventures in Wonderland*, the author Lewis Carrol writes of a scene where Alice comes to a crossroads and meets Cheshire the Cat:

> *"Would you tell me, please, which way I ought to go from here?" asked Alice.*
>
> *"That depends a good deal on where you want to get to," said the Cat.*
>
> *"I don't much care where–" said Alice.*
>
> *"Then it doesn't matter which way you go," said the Cat.[1]*

HOW MUCH DO YOU WANT A NEW DIRECTION?

You must make a decision. Joshua at the end of his life laid a very potent challenge to his heirs:

> But if serving the LORD seems undesirable to you, then choose for yourselves this day whom you will serve, whether the gods your forefathers served beyond the River, or the gods of the Amonites, in whose land you are living. But as for me and my household, we will serve the Lord. (Joshua 24:15, NIV)

Let us choose our direction wisely and know where we want to go!

DESIRE IS NOT ABILITY, BUT IT IS A GOOD BEGINNING

Most summers my family and I will travel to our favorite vacation spot way up in Moosehead Lake, Maine. We camp twenty miles from the nearest town, and there is no cell phone or internet connection. It's beautiful, remote, and out of reach for most people to find. We see moose, bear, deer and coyote.

One lazy, sunny day, we decided that we wanted to visit another remote camp, but we were not sure how to get there. It didn't seem too far on the map, so we asked our host for directions, and he abruptly retorted, "You can't get there from here!"

We knew that the lake itself is over forty miles long with many islands and impossible terrain. But, we weren't swimming, we were driving and determined! After many hours of riding deep into the wilderness on back dirt roads covered with potholes the size of small cars and skirting fallen trees lying across the primitive access route, we did in fact get to the other camp. It was rough and definitely rustic. We decided that the journey was certainly worth the effort. We could, in fact, get there from where we were!

We had the desire, but it took some muster to get there! Mission accomplished!

The enemy of our soul would have us believe that breaking our habits and sinful behavior is impossible; we can't get there from here! At times, we feel so overwhelmed by our own shortcomings, habits, and sins that we don't know if we can ever change. We wonder if it's possible!

After all, why do we struggle with habits and behaviors that are so contrary to what we know we should be doing? Doesn't the Bible make it seem as though I should be able to simply overcome? After all, don't some of the sermons on Sunday often reinforce that idea?

It really should be that simple – but is it?

Please remember this: Simply stated does not mean simply lived!

Desire is not ability! It's a great place to start, but not a great place to park.

It is helpful to read about the Apostle Paul's struggle.

He nailed this very dilemma when he wrote the book of Romans. He described his own troubled heart. Can you relate to his frustrations?

I do not understand what I do. For what I want to do I do not do, but what I hate I do." (Romans 7:15, NIV)

Then again he states:

For what I do is not the good I want to do; no, the evil I do not want to do--this I keep on doing. (Romans 7:19, NIV)

Then to further punctuate his frustration he declares:

What a wretched man I am! Who will rescue me from this body that is subject to death? (Romans 7:24, NIV)

The Apostle Paul did not leave us with his own frustrations without an answer to this dilemma. He stated on the heels of his exasperation an extraordinary declaration:

Thanks be to God, who delivers me through Jesus Christ our Lord! (Romans 7:25, NIV)

ONE OF THE MOST DIFFICULT QUESTIONS IN THE BIBLE

Some years ago I was moaning to myself over various things that I did not like in my character and lifestyle. I had been praying about some of these shortcomings when I read the story in John 5 of the lame man at the pool. This is a story most of us know well, and perhaps we have heard some good sermons on this passage of scripture. However, that day it became personal for me!

Now there is in Jerusalem near the Sheep Gate a pool, which in Aramaic is called Bethesda and which is surrounded by five covered colonnades. Here a great number of disabled people used to lie—the blind, the lame, the paralyzed.

One who was there had been an invalid for thirty-eight years. When Jesus saw him lying there and learned that he had been in this condition for a long time, he asked him, "Do you want to get well?"

"Sir," the invalid replied, "I have no one to help me into the pool when the water is stirred. While I am trying to get in, someone

else goes down ahead of me."

Then Jesus said to him, "Get up! Pick up your mat and walk."

At once the man was cured; he picked up his mat and walked. The day on which this took place was a Sabbath, (John 5:2-9, NIV)

The magnitude of conviction that slammed into me was overwhelming!

I had to face a very hard question "Do you want to get well?"

Did I read that correctly?

Jesus seems quite harsh! This man had not walked in thirty-eight years! Was it not terribly insensitive and insulting to ask such a question - "Do you want to get well?"

When I read this Scripture through the lens of my personal experience of frustration, I realized that I, like the lame man, wanted to cover my tracks with excuses! In fact, like me, many men have created an entire identity – a lame persona if you will, that shelters them from any real change.

We play the "Poor me, I'm addicted" role!

We claim we know where we want to go with God and that we desire to change, but the truth exposes our crafty lopsided lies and excuses.

Jesus gives us nowhere to run! Do we want to get well?

More specifically, "Do YOU want to get well?"

While I recognize that addictions are very real, I have often wondered if we have created a safe shelter in the name of "addictions" that require nothing but moaning and produce no real change. In fact, we adopt a label and identity that God never intended.

I wonder if many men have assured themselves that someday Jesus will deliver them of their entrenched patterns of thinking and actions.

Do they feel that until He does, they are stuck with this dysfunctional, sinful, and debilitating lifestyle?

I had to come clean! I had created all kinds of bogus arguments as to why I was allowed to live the way I lived. I was, after all, another victim in society just trying to have God help me in my life! What hellish lies! The words of Jesus were bursting in my ears, "DO YOU WANT TO GET WELL?"

ACTUALLY, YOU CAN GET THERE FROM HERE!

It is utterly bizarre to imagine a ten to twenty day walking journey from Egypt to the "Promise Land" taking forty years! The children of Israel would eventually get to where they wanted to go. They certainly had desire! But, they had to face the facts.

They were not prepared spiritually. They lacked the spiritual ability to handle the journey!

The "Promise Land" was not simply given to them at a rewards ceremony by their enemies! It was fought for every inch of the way! They finally knew what they wanted, and they knew how to get there, but it would be won one battle at a time. They were honing in on the skills required both spiritually and physically for all the Lord had intended!

More often than not, we have to "man up" and fight the good fight, removing weak arguments and clichés as to why we allow ourselves to remain near the pool but not in it; wandering near the "Promise Land", but not possessing it! God's promises are yea and amen!

TIME FOR A NEW DIRECTION!

Had my father not opened the hood of my car and worked on the engine, I would have gone nowhere! I tried to help my dad, and I know he appreciated it, but I was not the expert - he was. He fixed that Opel and made it run like new!

That's what our Heavenly Father does! He opens the hood and gets into our souls and begins to change the bad parts and replace them with the new ones.

The secular world offers "behavior modification," but the Lord offers "new creation."

> *Therefore, if anyone is in Christ, the new creation has come: The old has gone, the new is here!* (2 Corinthians 5:17, NIV).

The Lord has the power because He is Spirit!

What does that mean?

Everything in this world is material of some kind! Even the atoms and gases are made up of matter in some form. All that exists has come from Spirit, and God created everything according to Genesis 1.

This truth shows us that the Spirit is more powerful than matter and material. Everything we deal with in this life is wrapped into some piece of matter or material. If the Lord created all that is, He is competent to get under the hood and fix what needs fixing because He is more powerful than the matter or material that He created and that keeps us jammed up and enslaved!

> *'Not by might nor by power, but by my Spirit,' says the Lord Almighty.* (Zechariah 4:6, NIV)

Breaking entrenched patterns of behavior can be accomplished if we embrace and act upon the following:

1. PROCESS

Recognize that the intent of the heart is evil and that hiding behind excuses that permit an unholy lifestyle is utterly deceptive.

The Word of God says:

> *The heart is deceitful above all things and beyond cure. Who can understand it?* (Jeremiah 17:9, NIV)

Embrace His truth! The Lord is working on you! Allow the Holy

Spirit to speak to your shortcomings. The Lord wants to "open your hood" through the reading of the Bible and fervent prayer (James 5:16), so that He can work deep inside you - so you can get well!

2. PATIENCE

Be kind to yourself! God has not given up on you! If He had, you wouldn't be reading this book!

You are on the journey of faith. The Lord is your guide. The Word of God says,

> *Be assured that the testing of your faith [through experience] produces endurance [leading to spiritual maturity, and inner peace]. And let endurance have its perfect result and do a thorough work, so that you may be perfect and completely developed [in your faith], lacking in nothing.* (James 1:3-4, Amplified Version)

3. PERSISTENCE

Remember the old saying, "Behold the turtle; he makes progress only when he sticks out his neck!"[2]

Don't buy the lie of the enemy! Remember another old saying, "Quitters never win and winners never quit!"[3]

Remember, you are moving forward in the right direction because you know where you want to go! Don't withdraw into your old self again. Stick out your neck and move forward.

The Lord is giving you the power and ability to overcome!

> *Being confident of this, that he who began a good work in you will carry it on to completion until the day of Christ Jesus.* (Philippians 1:6 ,NIV)

4. *POWER*

Refuse to buy into an identity that God has not ascribed to you!

Do you want to get well? Yes, you do!

The Word of God says:

> *Call to Me, and I will answer you, and show you great and mighty things, which you do not know.* (Jeremiah 33:3, NKJV)

Your power is inadequate to break addictive cycles. If we cooperate with the Lord, however, He will radically change and empower us! We dare not trust in our own strength:

> *This is what the Lord says: "Cursed is the one who trusts in man, who draws strength from mere flesh and whose heart turns away from the Lord. That person will be like a bush in the wastelands; they will not see prosperity when it comes. They will dwell in the parched places of the desert, in a salt land where no one lives.*
>
> *But blessed is the one who trusts in the Lord, whose confidence is in him. They will be like a tree planted by the water that sends out its roots by the stream. It does not fear when heat comes; its leaves are always green. It has no worries in a year of drought and never fails to bear fruit."* (Jeremiah 17:5-8, NIV)

5. PASSION

What are you passionate about?

I know men that are avid hunters! They love it! Others love to golf, watch football, baseball, soccer, basketball, etc.

How about turning up the heat on your commitment and becoming passionate for Jesus!

You got it – a major Jesus freak!

Until you develop a real passion for Jesus Christ, His people, and the Word, you're just spinning wheels! Addiction to Jesus can break any addiction on the planet!

Isn't it time? Let the Lord get under your hood! He is leading you – let Him - you can get there from here!

BIG IDEA:

In order to become the man of God we were created to be, we need to realize the need to break the sinful, destructive cycles in our lives. Only then can we gain victory and overcome.

GROUP STUDY QUESTIONS:

1. Do you want to break the cycle of sin in your life?

2. The author discussed the need to stop covering our sin with excuses. What excuses do you use to cover sins?

3. What role does the Holy Spirit play in our breaking cycles?

4. The author discussed patience and realizing the need to be kind to ourselves as we persist through, towards freedom. How is this different than covering our tracks with excuses?

5. What is your level of passion for Jesus? Are there other things you're more passionate about? Why?

6. After reading this chapter, what is one thing you will put into practice or one thing you will change in your life?

7. How can we, as a group, help you do this?

2

OVERCOMING COMPROMISE

By Shawn Bentley

"Elijah was a human being, even as we are. He prayed earnestly that it would not rain, and it did not rain on the land for three and a half years."

(James 5:17, NIV)

Elijah was one of the greatest prophets of the Bible. He is the one who stood before King Ahab and said:

> *As the Lord, the God of Israel, lives, whom I serve, there will be neither dew nor rain in the next few years except at my word.* (1 Kings 17:1, NIV)

Elijah was a "blood and guts" kind of guy. He was the guy who climbed Mount Carmel for a "fire from heaven" showdown with the priests of Baal.

He was the guy who said to the people:

> *How long will you waver between two opinions? If the Lord is God, follow him; but if Baal is God, follow him.* (1 Kings 18:21, NIV)

Elijah. When his life's work was over, he was the one who was caught up in the whirlwind and took a ride on a chariot of fire sent by God.

When Jesus was on the earth, Elijah and Moses were the guys who God chose to meet and talk with Christ on the Mount of Transfiguration.

Listen to what God says in Malachi 4:5-6:

> See, I will send the prophet Elijah to you before that great and dreadful day of the Lord comes. He will turn the hearts of the parents to their children, and the hearts of the children to their parents..." (NIV)

Elijah, the prophet of God, was an incredible man! And yet, there is this amazing statement in James 5:17 that says:

> Elijah was a man with a nature like ours. (NIV)

The phrase, "with a nature like ours," is only used one time in the entire Bible.

What does James mean when he says, "Elijah was a man with a nature like ours"?

I have a little trouble understanding that. Can you picture Elijah facing some of the situations you face? Can you see him in some of the relationships you have? Hard to imagine, isn't it? Yet, James says that "Elijah was a man with a nature like ours."

If James had said that Peter was a man with a nature like ours, I wouldn't have had a problem with that at all. Peter often said the wrong thing, talking when he should have kept quiet and fighting the plan of God with bullheaded stubbornness!

Of course, I could see how David was a man with a nature like ours. David writes of his frustrations, searching for God's will and questioning who he can trust. David had trouble with his kids. David struggled with lust. Plainly put, David sinned. David was a man with a nature like ours.

But James says, "Elijah was a man with a nature like ours."

James brings Elijah to the storyline to point out that God can take ordinary people and accomplish extraordinary things. Let's dig a little deeper and see what we can learn from Elijah's life.

"NO COMPROMISE" MUST BE A "BUILT-IN" MINDSET FOR THE MAN OF GOD

Elijah demonstrates how someone committed to God will not compromise his faith. Elijah believed with all his heart that Jehovah is God, and there is no other God. This brought him into a confrontation with King Ahab. Maybe you remember his wife better; her name was Jezebel.

King Ahab did evil in the eyes of God. Making matters worse, he married a woman who believed that Baal was God.

Ahab was a politician who didn't want to offend anybody, especially his wife Jezebel.

Ahab decided that if worshiping one God is good, then worshiping two gods is even better. So he built altars to Baal. He brought in priests of Baal and told the people, "You can worship whichever god you choose, or you can worship both of them if you want."

Elijah confronted Ahab and condemned his idolatry. As a result of Ahab's example, many of the Israelites were now worshiping Baal or both Baal and the Lord. They couldn't make up their minds.

Finally, Elijah calls for a showdown on Mount Carmel.

In 1 Kings 18:21 Elijah asks, *"How long will you waver between two opinions? If the Lord is God, follow him; but if Baal is God, follow him."* (NIV)

Elijah was saying, "You cannot serve both the Lord and Baal at the same time. So make up your minds which one you're going to worship."

Then he challenged the priests of Baal to a contest to see which god was actually able to answer prayer.

The priests of Baal built an altar. They called on Baal to send down fire from heaven. Nothing happened. They shouted, they tore their clothing, and even cut themselves, but nothing happened.

Finally, in the evening, when it was obvious that they had completely failed to get a response from Baal, Elijah said, "Now it is my turn."

It was time to let God be God; a time to prove once and for all who the one true God really is.

In 1 Kings 18:30 we read:

> *Then Elijah said to all the people, "Come here to me."' They came to him. Elijah rebuilds the altar of God, that had been long neglected, and offers his sacrifice upon it. (NIV)*

Then Elijah prays a personal, heartfelt prayer found in 1 Kings 18:36-37 (NIV). Here he prays:

> *Lord, the God of Abraham, Isaac and Israel, let it be known today that you are God in Israel and that I am your servant and have done all these things at your command. Answer me, Lord, answer me, so these people will know that you, Lord, are God, and that you are turning their hearts back again.*

God responds with fire from heaven to take that which was offered on the altar of sacrifice. The people respond crying out "*The Lord - He is God! The Lord - He is God!*"

There is a message here for men today.

Elijah's life said, "I will not compromise. I will keep my life focused on God. I will stand up for the fact that God is Who He is, Lord of my life!"

Elijah's life challenges us with this statement: "What you believe determines how you behave."

The world will tolerate you as a Christian man as long as you don't get too serious about it. Our culture today will say "You are free to believe whatever you like, just don't try and force it into my life."

Subjectivism - the belief that "I, the subject, have the right to determine what is right and wrong without submitting my judgment to any authority outside myself" - is as powerful now as it was then.

Today is the same as it was in I Kings 18 where they compromised and diluted the worship of God to the point where they were no longer paying any attention to the Word or the will of God. They compromised.

People may say, "Your god is as good as mine. You worship yours and I'll worship mine. It really doesn't make much difference."

Elijah's message for us today remains the same, "Serve the one true God without compromise!"

CONFORMED MAN OR TRANSFORMED MAN OF GOD?

In Romans 12:1-2, *Paul says, "Therefore, I urge you, brothers and sisters, in view of God's mercy, to offer your bodies as a living sacrifice, holy and pleasing to God—this is your true and proper worship. Do not conform to the pattern of this world, but be transformed by the renewing of your mind. Then you will be able to test and approve what God's will is—his good, pleasing and perfect will." (NIV)*

Conform or transform.

As you study the Bible and read about the impact made by the people in its stories, you'll find that those people fit into one of two categories: those who conformed to their world, and those who transformed their world.

Ananias and Sapphira conformed.

Sure, they went to church; they said their prayers. They were a part of the church; they were respected in the church. However, they desired to be praised, and they ended up lying to the Holy Spirit.

Judas conformed.

He had the privilege of listening to the teachings of Jesus

Himself, yet he conformed and sold out to the world for money.

Joseph in the Old Testament didn't conform.

He was sold into slavery. He was tempted to commit adultery with Potiphar's wife. But he didn't conform to the world; instead he transformed the world in which he lived.

Daniel did not conform.

He wouldn't conform to the food at the table. He wouldn't bow down to the idols when so many others would. He kept on believing and praying even though it took him through a den of lions!

The same is true of so many others that have allowed God to transform their lives. The pressures to compromise were there, yet they would not conform. God used them in powerful ways as He transformed others through them.

In Matthew 6:24, Jesus said, *"No one can serve two masters. Either you will hate the one and love the other, or you will be devoted to the one and despise the other. You cannot serve both God and money."* (NIV)

We live in a culture of compromise. There are other altars and other gods calling for our attention and our worship. Society says, "That's all right. You can go to church and be a respectable Christian. Just go ahead and serve the other gods too."

Paul blueprints a different building code: *"Don't conform, but be transformed."* And here's how: *"Offer your bodies as living sacrifices. Give yourself to God."*

RENEW YOUR MIND

Let God's Word teach you and shape your thinking, your attitudes, and your values.

> *Then you will be able to test and approve what God's will is—his good, pleasing and perfect will for your life.* (Romans 12:2, NIV)

God has a plan for you. Don't compromise it!

Like Elijah, stand strong on the foundation God has already established.

For God so loved the world that he gave his one and only Son, that whoever believes in him shall not perish but have eternal life. For God did not send his Son into the world to condemn the world, but to save the world through him. (John 3:16, 17, NIV)

BIG IDEA:

The world constantly tries to get God's men to conform to their ways through compromise. We need to allow God's Word and God's power to transform us into the men God wants us to be!

GROUP STUDY QUESTIONS:

1. How are you tempted to compromise your faith?

2. The author says, "The world will tolerate you as a Christian man as long as you don't get too serious about it." What does this mean?

3. How do we avoid letting the world define how far we go for God?

4. What is the difference between being conformed and transformed?

5. What are steps you can take to make sure you are transformed, not conformed?

6. After reading this chapter, what is one thing you will put into practice or one thing you will change in your life?

7. How can we, as a group, help you do this?

OVERCOMING ANGER

By: David Kennard

I learned a long time ago that my spiritual well-being and my spiritual growth is a large part the result of how I think. It's the same for you! As a follower of Jesus, you are the product of your thoughts.

The writer of Proverbs 23:7 says:

For as he thinks in his heart, so is he. (NKJV)

It's not as we "feel."

You can't trust your emotions – they are fickle.

That's why it's important that we understand that when it comes to dealing with anger, the issue is not "how do you feel?"

The real issue is, "What do you think?" The scary thing is that our culture is not into thinking. We are more concerned about feelings and success. Let me put it this way: People today don't ask, "Is it true or is it right?" They ask, "Will it work? And how will it make me feel?" They don't know if it's right, and they don't care if it's right. They are only into feeling. And as a result, we are living in a society that is led by its feelings.

The problem is that your feelings come and go, and your feelings can deceive you. You can feel a certain way one time and a certain way another time.

However, if you are going to have stability and spiritual growth in your life, you can't be true to your feelings. You must be true to your convictions.

Your convictions are based on what you think! That's why the way you think is critical!

God is concerned with how you think. In fact, He calls us to think:

> *"Come now, and let us reason together," says the Lord, "Though your sins are as scarlet, they will be as white as snow; though they are red like crimson, they will be like wool."* (Isaiah 1:18, NASB)

God didn't say, "Come let us feel this ..." Or, "Come let us experience this ..." He said, "Let us reason!" The Bible calls you to think!

> *I will instruct you and teach you in the way you should go; I will counsel you with my loving eye on you. Do not be like the horse or the mule, which have no understanding but must be controlled by bit and bridle or they will not come to you.* (Psalms 32:8–9, NIV)

God is saying, "I'll give you truth and instruction."

How you think will have a huge influence on your stability! Faith is based on thought. It is not an irrational belief. It is a reasonable trust in the revealed truth about the true God! So if you want to be stable, you must think correctly.

My goal is to help you see what the Bible says specifically about anger. To be honest, this is one of the signature sins that I struggle with in an ongoing way. So what I'm sharing with you comes from a place of weakness rather than from a guy who has totally mastered the way I overcome anger. The Holy Spirit is still working in my life in these areas, and for that I'll be forever grateful.

If you wrestle with your temper, perhaps you can relate to the struggle that is anger.

Anger has a way of messing us up. It can steal your inner peace. It can wreck your relationships, and it can wreck your home. Anger can destroy you and ruin your future.

Don't let it! Determine right now, as you work through these thoughts, to allow the Holy Spirit to shape you into a person who is calm.

REALIZE THE COST OF ANGER

Anger will cost you when you are given to fits of rage. When you don't control your temper, it will leave relational carnage behind. The writers of Scripture knew that:

> *A quick-tempered person does foolish things, and the one who devises evil schemes is hated.* (Proverbs 14:17, NIV)

If you're a guy with a hot temper, you will do foolish things.

> *A hot-tempered person stirs up conflict, but the one who is patient calms a quarrel.* (Proverbs 15:18, NIV)

A good way to get into a fight is to have a quick temper and just fly off the handle.

> *A hot-tempered person must pay the penalty; rescue them, and you will have to do it again.* (Proverbs 19:19, NIV)

When you fly into a rage, there is always a penalty, and there is so much you can lose. You can lose your friends, job, and relationship with your family. You can also distance yourself from God when you lose your temper. Every time you get angry, you lose. You risk losing some of the things God has given you.

Moses learned the cost of anger. He was not a man that you

would normally think of as being a hot-head. But Moses never really learned to control his temper.

> *One day, after Moses had grown up, he went out to where his own people were and watched them at their hard labor. He saw an Egyptian beating a Hebrew, one of his own people. Looking this way and that and seeing no one, he killed the Egyptian and hid him in the sand.* (Exodus 2:11–12, NIV)

It was an unreasonable act being committed against a Hebrew. And Moses was filled with fury.

> *At that time Moses was born, and he was no ordinary child. For three months he was cared for by his family. When he was placed outside, Pharaoh's daughter took him and brought him up as her own son. Moses was educated in all the wisdom of the Egyptians and was powerful in speech and action.*
>
> *When Moses was forty years old, he decided to visit his own people, the Israelites. He saw one of them being mistreated by an Egyptian, so he went to his defense and avenged him by killing the Egyptian.* (Acts 7:20–24, NIV)

Notice that it says Moses was highly educated. Education does not necessarily reduce anger. You can be highly educated and still have a temper. Still, he was taking vengeance into his own hands, so Moses was sent to the desert for forty years to "cool his jets." He had learned a lot, but he hadn't learned how to handle his temper.

Between the ninth and tenth plagues, Moses visited Pharaoh. By that time he was absolutely put out with Pharaoh – even though God had told him that Pharaoh would harden his heart.

> *So Moses said, "This is what the Lord says: 'About midnight I will go throughout Egypt. Every firstborn son in Egypt will die, from the firstborn son of Pharaoh, who sits on the throne, to the firstborn son of the female slave, who is at her hand mill, and all the firstborn of the cattle as well. There will be loud wailing throughout Egypt—worse than there has ever been or ever will be again. But among the Israelites not a dog will bark at any person or animal.'*

Then you will know that the Lord makes a distinction between Egypt and Israel. All these officials of yours will come to me, bowing down before me and saying, 'Go, you and all the people who follow you!'

After that I will leave."Then Moses, hot with anger, left Pharaoh. (Exodus 11:4–8, NIV)

That means what it says. Those are the strongest words that one can use to express anger. He was ticked off!

My question is: "Moses, why are you mad? God told you Pharaoh wouldn't respond. You don't need to get mad; just give him the message."

But Moses wasn't content just to give it. He had to give it in anger!

Let's go a step further ... when we pick up the story in Exodus 32, the people were at Mount Sinai. Moses was up on the mountain. The people got tired of waiting. They said: "We don't know what has happened to Moses." So they built a calf. And Moses came down from the mountain.

Moses turned and went down the mountain with the two tablets of the covenant law in his hands. They were inscribed on both sides, front and back. The tablets were the work of God; the writing was the writing of God, engraved on the tablets.

When Joshua heard the noise of the people shouting, he said to Moses, "There is the sound of war in the camp."

Moses replied: "It is not the sound of victory, it is not the sound of defeat; it is the sound of singing that I hear."

When Moses approached the camp and saw the calf and the dancing, his anger burned and he threw the tablets out of his hands, breaking them to pieces at the foot of the mountain. (Exodus 32:15–19, NIV)

You say, "Well, shouldn't he have gotten angry?"

Absolutely, there is such a thing as righteous indignation. Anger is not necessarily sinful.

But notice what Moses did in verse 19:

> When Moses approached the camp and saw the calf and the dancing, his anger burned and he threw the tablets out of his hands, breaking them to pieces at the foot of the mountain.

He took those documents written by the very finger of God, and in a moment of rage, he smashed them. It was simply an act of temper.

And if you will read the account, you will find that God never verbally justified or commended Moses' action. God never bragged on Moses for doing that. In fact, look at what God said when Moses got the law a second time in Exodus 34:1:

> The Lord said to Moses, "Chisel out two stone tablets like the first ones, and I will write on them the words that were on the first tablets, which you broke." (Exodus 34:1, NIV)

One final example is found in the book of Numbers. The children of Israel had been wandering in the desert for thirty-nine years. And they had complained every step of the way. Moses was tired of it and was on the edge of irritation.

> In the first month the whole Israelite community arrived at the Desert of Zin, and they stayed at Kadesh. There Miriam died and was buried. Now there was no water for the community, and the people gathered in opposition to Moses and Aaron. They quarreled with Moses and said, "If only we had died when our brothers fell dead before the Lord! Why did you bring the Lord's community into this wilderness, that we and our livestock should die here? Why did you bring us up out of Egypt to this terrible place? It has no grain or figs, grapevines or pomegranates. And there is no water to drink!"
>
> Moses and Aaron went from the assembly to the entrance to the tent of meeting and fell facedown, and the glory of the Lord appeared to them. The Lord said to Moses, "Take the staff, and you and your brother Aaron gather the assembly together. Speak

to that rock before their eyes and it will pour out its water. You will bring water out of the rock for the community so they and their livestock can drink."

So Moses took the staff from the Lord's presence, just as he commanded him. He and Aaron gathered the assembly together in front of the rock and Moses said to them, "Listen, you rebels, must we bring you water out of this rock?"

Then Moses raised his arm and struck the rock twice with his staff. Water gushed out, and the community and their livestock drank.

But the Lord said to Moses and Aaron, "Because you did not trust in Me enough to honor Me as holy in the sight of the Israelites, you will not bring this community into the land I give them." (Numbers 20:1–12, NIV)

Wait a minute, Moses, where is that in God's instructions?

You see, burning with anger, he took advantage of the situation to tell the people off. "Must we bring you water!" And in anger, he lifted up his rod and struck that rock. Not once and not lightly. It wasn't a tap.

God had said, "Speak to it." It was a fit of rage, and it cost him!

And you may think that Moses shrugged it off, but three times in Deuteronomy Moses asked God to overlook it until finally God said, "Don't ask again ... the answer is "no":

But because of you the Lord was angry with me and would not listen to me. "That is enough," the Lord said. "Do not speak to Me anymore about this matter." (Deuteronomy 3:26, NIV)

Because of anger, Moses was not allowed into the Promised Land.

Guys, learn the lesson now – anger will cost you!

RECOGNIZE THE CAUSE OF ANGER

What causes anger?

You say, "When people do stupid things I get angry."

No, that's not the cause of your anger. That's your response to anger. But anger is caused by certain things. What is the process of anger?

> *'In your anger do not sin': Do not let the sun go down while you are still angry, and do not give the devil a foothold.* (Ephesians 4:26–27, NIV)

Sometimes you go to bed angry with your wife, kids, employer, employee, friends, etc. Yet what you may not realize is that anger erodes your soul.

When you go to bed angry, do you know what is happening? Do you know what you are saying?

You are saying, "Devil you are welcome to come and wreck my home, my happiness, my testimony, and destroy my life." And that stubborn anger becomes the beachhead from which the devil will attack and take more and more ground.

There are several steps to disaster when you become engulfed with anger:

> *Get rid of all bitterness, rage and anger, brawling and slander, along with every form of malice.* (Ephesians 4:31, NIV)

Let's look at what a few of those words mean:

---Bitterness is the feeling of resentment that we get when we think that we have been wronged. Somebody did something. Somebody said something.

---Bitterness turns to rage. Inside we begin to burn. At this point you're "hot and bothered".

---Anger refers to the outward manifestation. What we have on the inside begins to show on the outside ... in the way we talk ... in the way we drive, etc.

---Brawling is loud speech. We are angry, and suddenly we get loud. You say, "You don't have to shout!" And they say, "I'm not shouting!"

---Slander is saying things you shouldn't say. You say things that you don't mean. You say, "I hate you." "I wish we never would have started dating." "You'll never amount to anything." We say all kinds of things that even as they are being said we know that we don't mean them. And we have given the devil a foothold.

---Malice is the desire to hurt and to harm. You might hit, slap or get a gun. Or you can do it psychologically. But you desire to hurt people. And the whole time that is going on, guess who is standing in the corner and smiling - the enemy! It's all because you said, "Come on in."

That's the cause of anger. It's caused when we let these things reside in our hearts. It's caused when we don't deal with it immediately.

One final, really important caution: the people we hang around with can cause us to become prone to fits of anger.

> *Do not make friends with a hot-tempered person, do not associate with one easily angered, or you may learn their ways and get yourself ensnared.* (Proverbs 22:24–25, NIV)

If you hang around people who have temper tantrums, then you risk becoming like them. Pick your inner circle wisely!

REFUSE TO BE CONTROLLED BY ANGER

You say, "I can't control my anger!"

But you can!

Have you ever had one of those family discussions that were heated? Right in the middle, your phone rings; you answer and say, "Hello," and you sound so sweet. If you can't control your anger ... then why did you answer your phone so kindly? You CAN control it.

Look at these Scriptures:

> *Fools show their annoyance at once, but the prudent overlook an insult.* (Proverbs 12:16, NIV)

That means that you can do it.

> *Fools give full vent to their rage, but the wise bring calm in the end.* (Proverbs 29:11, NIV)

Guess what, this still means that you can do it. A wise person doesn't just spout things out. You control it.

> *Bridle your anger, trash your wrath, cool your pipes—it only makes things worse.* (Psalms 37:8, MSG)

Let's examine the life of a guy named Cain who didn't learn to control his anger. He found himself forever ruined because he was out of control.

> *In the course of time Cain brought some of the fruits of the soil as an offering to the Lord. And Abel also brought an offering—fat portions from some of the firstborn of his flock. The Lord looked with favor on Abel and his offering, but on Cain and his offering he did not look with favor.*
>
> *So Cain was very angry, and his face was downcast.*
>
> *Then the Lord said to Cain, "Why are you angry? Why is your face downcast? If you do what is right, will you not be accepted? But if you do not do what is right, sin is crouching at your door; it desires to have you, but you must rule over it".* (Genesis 4:3–7, NIV)

What happened with Cain and Abel doesn't happen overnight. There seems to be a slippery slope – a downhill progression that leads someone from anger to full blown murder.

It begins with our thought life. Anger turns to contempt and then hatred.

Bitterness begins to set in which leads to rage. This brewing, boiling anger lingers and moves into the realm of a revenge that will not be satisfied.

It moves from thoughts to words which find their expression in action. And before you know it, you snap and murder.

All of us would say, "I am NOT a murderer." But it's amazing how we can get so dangerously close to moving down this slope without even realizing it. What is it about your heart and mine that is so dark that we can be set off so quickly?

Isn't it true that we tend to get angry at God even when we're the ones not doing the right thing?

Don't be someone who deliberately disobeys God, and then turns around and gets mad at Him for not blessing you. If we'd just learn to do the right thing in every situation, we would save ourselves from a lot of problems and misplaced anger. The truth of the matter is that when we don't do what is right, sin is definitely crouching at our door. And it really does desire to have us.

Anger desires to have you, but YOU must master it! If you don't deal effectively with your lack of patience and self-control, it will tighten its grip around you and eventually destroy you. Cain caved in to anger and ended up a murderer.

You shall not murder. (Exodus 20:13, NIV)

You have heard that it was said to the people long ago, "You shall not murder, and anyone who murders will be subject to judgment." But I tell you that anyone who is angry with a brother or sister, will be subject to judgment. Again, anyone who says to a brother or sister, "Raca," is answerable to the court. And anyone who says, "You fool!" will be in danger of the fire of hell." (Matthew 5:21–22, NIV)

Jesus says, "You bought into this lie that as long as you do not take someone's life with your own hands you are alright. But I say, if you are angry and you hold someone in contempt or you think they are worthless then you are already guilty."

Now I would assume that we would all agree that there is a progression between our thoughts and our actions.

But what Jesus says is, "You are wrong. There is NO progression! There is NO slope! You are guilty of committing murder whether it's with your hands or your heart."

The brilliance of Jesus' teaching was this: If it is in your heart or in your brain, it counts. It's real, and it matters!

When you devalue or demean other people, you have crossed the line.

Murder is not just what you do. It's what you think, feel, and say.

When you mock others or assassinate their character, you are treating them with contempt. You are destroying their reputation.

When you say hateful things to your friends with anger in your heart, you not only damage them – you are harming your own soul too.

When you fight with your parents with hate in your heart, you are destroying them and mutilating your own spirit in the process.

And Jesus says, "You're in danger of the fire of hell!" when you have that kind of anger.

Jesus understands how these things work, and so He came to give us a better way of dealing with murder and anger. Jesus gives us some invaluable advice that's aimed at helping us avoid death.

> *Therefore, if you are offering your gift at the altar and there remember that your brother or sister has something against you, leave your gift there in front of the altar. First go and be reconciled to them; then come and offer your gift.* (Matthew 5:23–24, NIV)

WE must initiate reconciliation.

Notice that Jesus doesn't say, "If you remember that YOU have something against someone."

He isn't concerned with "your" anger here.

No, He deals with "YOUR" offense that has hurt others. Now Jesus does deal elsewhere with what we're to do when we've been wronged. When conflict arises between those in the family of God, Jesus gives us this counsel:

If your fellow believer sins against you, go and tell him in private what he did wrong. If he listens to you, you have helped that person to be your brother or sister again. (Matthew 18:15, NCV)

I even hesitate to mention that because we are so often focused on the wrong that has been done to us. Generally speaking, it's not our place to go to others and tell them how they were wrong or how they wronged us. That's God's job to point out their stuff to them. Not ours!

That doesn't mean what has been done to you doesn't hurt. And that it wasn't wrong. I'm not trying to excuse anyone for what they've said or done to you. But this commandment doesn't deal with them. It's about you and me. God says, "Do not murder." And we must take responsibility for our own anger.

If you have anger and resentment in your heart, God's solution is for you to talk to HIM about it. You need to admit your bitterness and rage and ask God to forgive you of those feelings. You must let go of your stuff. You have to acknowledge before God that it's not right and that it's destroying you. Ask God to help you!

Are you guilty of murder? Is anger rampant in your home? Has death been spread everywhere? Have you allowed bitterness and resentment to go unchecked so that now it is swelling up in your spirit and soul? Are you willing to initiate reconciliation? Do you need to go to someone and make things right?

REPENT OVER YOUR ANGER

Meditate on these verses. Memorize the ones that really speak to you at this stage of your spiritual journey.

---*Too much talk leads to sin. Be sensible and keep your mouth shut.* (Proverbs 10:19, NLT)

---*The mouth of the righteous is a fountain of life, but the mouth of the wicked conceals violence.* (Proverbs 10:11, NIV)

---*Those who guard their lips preserve their lives, those who speak rashly will come to ruin.* (Proverbs 13:3, NIV)

---*A gentle answer will calm a person's anger, but an unkind answer will cause more anger. Wise people use knowledge when they speak, but fools pour out foolishness.* (Proverbs 15:1-2, NCV)

---*It is hard to stop a quarrel once it starts, so don't let it begin.* (Proverbs 17:14, TLB)

---*It is to one's honor to avoid strife, but every fool is quick to quarrel.* (Proverbs 20:3, NIV)

---*Do you see a man hasty in his words? There is more hope for a fool than for him.* (Proverbs 29:20, NKJV)

---*Let all bitterness, wrath, anger, clamor, and evil speaking be put away from you, with all malice. And be kind to one another, tenderhearted, forgiving one another, just as God in Christ forgave you.* (Ephesians 4:31-32, NKJV)

---*Everything you say should be kind and well thought out so that you know how to answer everyone.* (Colossians 4:6, GW)

---*Understand this, my dear brothers and sisters: You must all be quick to listen, slow to speak, and slow to get angry.* (James 1:19, NLT)

---*Don't repay evil for evil. Don't retaliate with insults when people insult you. Instead, pay them back with a blessing. That is what God has called you to do, and he will bless you for it.* (1 Peter 3:9, NLT)

It's not always a sin to be angry. Jesus was angry. You say, "What is the difference?"

> *He looked around at them in anger and, deeply distressed at their stubborn hearts, said to the man, "Stretch out your hand." He stretched it out, and his hand was completely restored.* (Mark 3:5, NIV)

Jesus was never angry over what someone did to Him. He never retaliated when people did things to Him. He always returned good for evil. He never tried to get even. But what angered Jesus was when people selfishly ran over other people and hurt them.

If your anger is over something that was done to you, it is not a righteous indignation. Hence, you need to recognize it for the sin that it is. Much of the anger we experience is sin.

> *The acts of the flesh are obvious: sexual immorality, impurity and debauchery; idolatry and witchcraft; hatred, discord, jealousy, fits of rage, selfish ambition, dissensions, factions and envy; drunkenness, orgies, and the like. I warn you, as I did before, that those who live like this will not inherit the kingdom of God.* (Galatians 5:19–21, NIV)

Until you go to God and admit that you have a problem, you're going to be plagued by guilt, regret and strained relationships.

Until you go to the people whom you have blown up at and admit you have a problem ... you will battle with anger.

Stop blaming it on your boss, wife, kids, pastor, or your stressful situation. It is your problem...confess it. And ask God to help you!

> *If we confess our sins, he is faithful and just and will forgive us our sins and purify us from all unrighteousness.* (1 John 1:9, NIV)

Don't delay in agreeing with God that your anger is a problem. Once you admit that to yourself, to Him and then to others you will begin to see the power of that signature sin broken in your life.

It's humbling, but totally worth the effort to get free of the bondage of an explosive temper!

BIG IDEA:

Anger will ruin you ... if you don't bring it under control. Pursue your Heavenly Father's nature and follow Jesus' example. Embrace love and choose to let go of your fury.

GROUP STUDY QUESTIONS:

1. What made you realize that anger was costing you something?

2. What relationships has your anger damaged?

3. In what situations do you feel most tempted to become angry?

4. In what relationships do you feel most tempted to become angry?

5. Who do you tend to blame your anger on the most?

6. Are you willing to initiate reconciliation? Do you need to go to someone and make things right?

7. What righteous anger do you experience?

AN UNEXAMINED LIFE

By Tony Cruz

Have you ever walked off a cliff? More specifically, have you ever jumped into a pit over 430 feet deep?

I am going to guess probably not.

But what if it happened to you when you weren't expecting it?

I'm sure it would do more than mess up your day---it probably would be a life changing moment!

You might wonder under what scenario this would happen.

The answer is: the natural phenomenon of sinkholes.

Sinkholes tend to appear suddenly and happen all over the world. They usually begin with an innocuous leak in a rusty pipe under the surface of the ground. The earth beneath your feet quietly erodes until one-day the bottom drops out. Whole buildings have been sucked into sinkholes. Entire roads have been knocked out and neighborhoods left devastated.

The largest natural sinkhole in the world, the Quattara Depression, measures over 260 feet long and 436 feet deep. It is located in Cairo, Egypt. This enormous sinkhole is both shocking and dangerous. Honestly, it's hard to believe that it was once flat land. Yet below the surface, something wasn't right. Something got past the officials, and it went unexamined.

Truth be told, an unexamined life can bring about all kinds of sinkholes that will seem to come out of nowhere but were happening in a place that is unseen. This can and will keep us from the prize. Allow me to explain.

Unexamined lives are untested lives. We can assume, project and even approximate but never fully "know." Then BOOM, a sinkhole hits, and we wonder, "Where did that come from?"

For each of us, an unexamined life brings with it certain sinkholes. But there is good news.

There are signs that help us catch them early and detect these spiritual sinkholes, before they cause catastrophic issues. Allow me to share some tips on how to catch this early and avoid much unnecessary pain.

FIND THE PROPER INSPECTORS

One thing that should be mentioned is that most sinkholes are not like the one mentioned at the beginning of this chapter. A sinkhole doesn't have to be a crater that can consume your entire house. A much smaller, less noticeable sinkhole can also do its fair share of harm, undermining your foundation and wreaking havoc with your plumbing.[1]

Most sinkholes are 10-12 feet in diameter. While this is significantly smaller in size, it doesn't change the fact that if one is at the wrong place at the wrong time, it can bring about serious, even fatal consequences.

Often the first way to avoid the crisis of a sinkhole is to have the right inspectors in place. These inspectors see the signs before others can. Because sinkholes and cracks can appear suddenly, it is vital to have people in place that can survey the land and ensure the warning signs are addressed.

There are many reasons why some people choose to examine their lives while others choose not to examine them at all. Some individuals do not examine their lives because of the fear of getting hurt or possibly a chance of failure. These lives are prime sinkhole candidates. This is a serious matter because men are prime targets of spiritual sinkholes. A little allowance of this and a little compromise of that and POOF, your house is gone!

Many men have a real fear of accountability. The need for "advice" is difficult because men don't want to appear to be any less "macho" than anyone else. Men in general have a hard time finding "inspector"-like friends who are willing to catch the signs before leading to disastrous repercussions.

I believe God is looking for individuals who are willing to examine the areas of life that really matter, the places deep inside that most people wouldn't notice or know is happening in you. Guys, this self-examination is important because your private life will be revealed in your public life eventually.

Accountability is a key part of an examined life. You will only hold yourself accountable for goals that others know about. Tell someone what you are up to! Passion without accountability is the equivalent of love without strategy.

It takes courage to be willing to be vulnerable. Courage starts by overcoming your fear of having your motives, your methods, and your mindset examined.

If you consider yourself a person of faith, get into a fellowship of believers who you can can connect with weekly, whether it's in a home or a building on Sunday. Here's a tip: don't leave it to just Sunday; that is not enough. You need more than a Sunday and more than a sermon. You need a "someone," maybe even a coach or a mentor.

Everyone needs that "someone" from time to time to tell you, "I don't believe that is what God intended for you" so you would not go back to your personal Egypt.

When we read about Egypt in the Old Testament of the Bible, it is often a symbol of our old life. Egypt is familiar, and we embrace the familiar very well and very quickly. We do this whenever we decide that familiarity is more important than breakthrough and FREEDOM!

Don't settle for comfort over conviction.

When you are in a constant state of comfort, you probably aren't being challenged or examined by others.

Don't fear examination. It will make you stronger in whatever you do. Call it constructive criticism or whatever you decide to call it, but in the end, you are the beneficiary. Accountability is living life insurance that you can collect while still here on this earth!

"A Life Examined is a Life that is Excelling".

It's also very important that each of us examine our lives against the truth of the Word of God.

The book of Romans tells us this hard truth:

> *...Let God be true, and every human being a liar...* (Romans 3:4, NIV)

As you try to follow Jesus, you will hear voices that tell you, "Just go back," or "You don't need this." Don't listen to them.

It's easy to listen to the other voices because there are so many that sound alike. Yet the hard truth is that they won't make you better. Instead of following the flow of opinions and expectations of people, follow the truth of God and His Word. That is what will remain true in your life.

"It's not the voices you hear, but the voices that you obey that truly matter."

OBSERVE YOUR SITE

In my research, I found that other signs of a sinkhole are slumping trees and/or falling longstanding fence posts that are usually sunk in deep. Other signs could be cracks in the interior walls of a home or even cracks in a street. These cracks show there is a separation happening that could be a long-term issue.

While it is true that we are not always at our best in observing and detecting these sinkholes, your failure isn't final. You will try and you will fall short; that is life. But those mistakes should not define you because you are being prepped for greatness.

Your life is always under construction. The temptation is to feel like your examination is a weakness.

On the contrary, it's a sign that your home and family are important to you. If you check your heart and your life, both you and your family will benefit.

Don't focus on failure or the possibility of it. There must be a point in life when you choose to chase the fear away or it will hurt you and affect every area of your life.

An unexamined life wants you to avoid yielding to anything that may bring you to a place of vulnerability. The fear of vulnerability will stall your growth and impede your family from seeing the true and living God because you are too busy looking at the sinkhole that was never attended to!

Numbers 14:2-3 tells us something powerful:

> *All the Israelites grumbled against Moses and Aaron, and the whole assembly said to them, "If only we had died in Egypt! Or in this wilderness! Why is the Lord bringing us to this land only to let us fall by the sword? Our wives and children will be taken as plunder. Wouldn't it be better for us to go back to Egypt?"* (NIV)

Here we see people chosen by God to be "His" and yet imperfect in every way possible.

God-given dreams intimidate many people.

Many give up on a dream for the convenient, logically achievable goal. The thought of "biting off more than I can chew" rattles people to their core, but who is doing the biting?

All God-given goals are done in His strength and might, so why try and rely so heavily on our own strength? More thought is given about the fear of failure than achieving that dream. This fear of where you are and where you are going causes many people to stutter step into mediocrity.

"Mediocrity is the casket where dreams go to die."

CHECK THE FOUNDATION

Did you know that a sinkhole doesn't need to be on your property to cause damage to your house? While researching sinkholes I learned that if there are signs of a sinkhole on a property near yours, you need to beware. Some experts even advise an inspection of your street.

Why go to so much trouble for a problem that isn't even on your property? Because long term it could affect your home's foundation. Your foundation is the key to your home being stable and safe from sinkholes.

In the same way, our faith is our foundation, and what we believe directly affects our stability. To make an impact on our homes, communities and world today, we must step outside of our borders to check the foundation.

Sinkholes are out there that have not been noticed! It takes courage to go beyond our borders. That courage is often not found alone. It is found with another individual that will cause you to see beyond your limited sight.

Sometimes you have to leave your "safe zone" to get into the "work zone" so that you can have a better situation. It is in that work zone that God begins to trim the old you to pull you out of your situation.

Stand still and do not fear. Everyone wants to get to the Promise Land but many never want to go through the wilderness just outside of that very same Promised Land.

For example, look at the Israelites in Numbers 14:2-4:

All the Israelites grumbled against Moses and Aaron, and the whole assembly said to them, "If only we had died in Egypt! Or in this wilderness! Why is the Lord bringing us to this land only to let us fall by the sword? Our wives and children will be taken as plunder. Wouldn't it be better for us to go back to Egypt?"

And they said to each other, "We should choose a leader and go back to Egypt." (NIV)

The Israelites began longing for the normalcy of slavery once again. To them, slavery in Egypt was normal. It was easier to take Israel out of Egypt, then to remove Egypt (the bondage mentality) out of Israel.

The challenge is to give someone the chance to walk alongside you who can help you see the Promised Land and avoid the sinkholes that destroy homes because of unexamined small leaks.

Small leaks make big heaps. The wrong friend online with unaccountable "browsing" is a small leak that can bring your life a world of hurt.

World-changing men need people with telescopes to tell them where they are going as well as others with a magnifying glass to tell them where they are presently.   With these tools, we can avoid the sinkholes in our lives.

BIG IDEA:

Unexamined lives are untested lives. For each of us, an unexamined life brings with it certain sinkholes. But there is good news. Through accountability and self-examination we can overcome the sinkholes in our lives and maintain a secure foundation.

GROUP STUDY QUESTIONS:

1. What is your most obvious sinkhole?

2. Do you have a "sinkhole inspector," someone who you allow to point out weak spots and danger zones in your life?

3. Why is self-examination, looking at your weak points and tendencies to sin, a sign of strength not weakness?

4. The author said, "Sometimes we need to step outside of our borders to check the foundation." What does this mean to you?

5. After reading this chapter, what is one thing you will put into practice or one thing you will change in your life?

6. How can we, as a group, help you do this?

-5-

OVERCOMING SEXUAL SIN

By Rob Stiem

We live in a sex-saturated culture where many have driven a long way down the road to "sexual freedom" only to find that road leads to pain and prison. The truths in this chapter are for those who've repeatedly compromised their walk with Christ by yielding to sexual sin, for anyone who finds they are heading that direction, or for anyone who's seeking to be a resource for someone who has already gone down this road.

If you are reading this, you are more than likely a Christ-professing man. But the reality is, this is an all-encompassing struggle from which any man, woman, or teen is capable of breaking free if they are willing to take the actions necessary for change.

Wherever you are in your spiritual journey and battle to overcome sexual sin, if you'll have a humble willingness to pray, *"God, I am a man under construction – help me to follow the scriptural blueprint for freedom laid out in the pages to follow,"* you can be confident He will use these truths as a tool of transformation. They will change your heart and mind and bring forgiveness, fresh hope, and true freedom into your life.

I cannot promise this change will happen overnight. The road to godliness and lasting freedom is most often a journey. It is a journey requiring discipline, sacrifice, time, accountability, surrender and dependence upon the Spirit's help, but the payoff is so worth it.

True freedom comes not from throwing off sexual restraints but from devoting ourselves to God's Word. By faith, King David's declaration can be your own:

> *I will walk about in freedom, for I have sought out your precepts.*
> (Psalm 119:45, NIV)

My own struggle to walk in the freedom of sexual purity began when I was eleven. One evening at my school, Fairplain East Elementary, we were putting on the fifth grade version of the musical "Mary Poppins." We were singing silly songs like "Supercalifragilisticexpialidocious" and "A Spoonful Of Sugar Makes the Medicine Go Down."

During the intermission, eight of us decided to go outside to the playground and burn off some energy. Unknown to us was that the outdoor movie theater right next to the school was playing a Triple X-rated movie. In the middle of running around, we stopped on a dime when we suddenly saw the porn images being displayed on the huge screen. So inside, we were performing Mary Poppins, and outside, our eyes were poppin' right out of our heads!

That messed my young mind up and caused me to begin sexualizing women. Though porn wasn't readily available then, I still found I could get lustful satisfaction from looking at scantily clad women in newspaper flyers, magazines, on the beach, or wherever I'd let my eyes wander. That was the start of an eight to ten year battle, in which I struggled to begin viewing women in a wholesome, biblical way – as deeply valued and loved by God and made in His image.

I'm so thankful for the work God did in my late teen years. He set me free and renewed my mind. He empowered me, through His Word and by the Holy Spirit, to fight and be victorious in the battle for purity in my thought life.

In my early 20's, I remember looking back with disgust and thinking "REALLY?" Who on earth allows a XXX movie to be shown next to an elementary school? What kind of messed up culture does that? But now, sadly, clips like the one I saw are being played daily and globally, thanks to the ease of Internet access.

Tragically, less than eleven-years-old has become the average at which children are first exposed to porn, and it is only trending younger.

As I found, porn truly messes up your mind and damages your soul. When you understand how God has wired the reward center of our brains to function, four things become evident.

Porn Exposes You – You cannot erase images from your mind, much less your soul.

Porn Numbs You - It's like a shot of Novocain to your spirit. While you may think it arouses you, the truth is, it deadens you. The more you see, the more it takes to excite you. It kills and deadens your spirit!

Porn Seduces You - It promises emotional and sexual satisfaction but never gives it. But it sure draws you in with the promise of it.

Porn is a Drug and Women are a Fantasy - "Gotta have that hit of dopamine" (the chemical released to the pleasure center of our brains when porn is viewed).

I've talked with dozens of men who've had substance abuse issues and have also struggled with porn addiction and most have relayed they've had more difficulty in becoming free from the prison of porn use than even their substance abuse.

Whether you're struggling with an addiction to porn, adultery, homosexuality or any other unwanted sexual behavior, God's Word gives us four truths that are crucial to overcoming sexual sin, pursuing purity and walking in freedom.

If you are going to walk in the freedom God offers, the first truth that is vital to understand is that:

YOUR SEXUALITY IS A GOD-CREATED, GOD-DESIGNED, HIGHLY-CHARGED DRIVE.

If this is misunderstood and not yielded to the Lordship of Jesus Christ, it will lead to great shame and pain, rather than the tremendous good and pleasure for which it was intended.

TREMENDOUS GOOD AND PLEASURE

Neither Hollywood nor the porn industry invented sex – God did! It was born in His heart and mind as a beautiful, passionate, self-giving way for a man and woman to express their deep love for one another. Through sexual intimacy, they give one another great pleasure, superglue their lives together and have children. Because God delights in His intended use of our sexuality, He had an entire book written about it. The Song of Solomon paints a captivating picture of the beauty and joy of marital sex between a husband and wife.

Sex is so much more than simply the physical act of uniting body parts; it is the interchange of the deepest part of ourselves; our spirit, soul and body. The boundaries God has given, for our sexuality to be expressed only within marriage, are for our protection, security and freedom – not to restrict us. He wants you to trust Him and discover that He is a loving, caring, faithful God Who wants your sexual needs met only in a good way that grows and nurtures you, not in ways that diminish, shame, or harm you.

GREAT PAIN AND SHAME

Because of the extensive misuse of this valuable gift, the reality is that the pain, shame and other negative consequences attached to sexual sin are widespread. The destructive nature is seen in God's command to run from sexual sin, because no other sin affects us as clearly as this one does. Sexual sin is the only sin listed in Scripture as *"a sin against our own bodies"* (1 Corinthians 6:18). Though not always immediately evident, our sexual sin also results in harmfully affecting those around us as well.

Each time you sin, you are playing ethical and moral Russian roulette with your life! So run, flee from sexual sin, because the life you save may very well be your own.

God's design for your sexuality is for your tremendous good and pleasure not for your pain or shame. God did not create you as a sexual being to cause you continual pain, shame and frustration. Whatever your sexual history is, God wants to give you a new perspective and a hope that this important area of your life can be one of tremendous good and pleasure as you bring your sexuality into alignment with His purposes and Word.

If you are going to overcome sexual sin and walk in the freedom God offers, the second vital truth to know is that:

HOLINESS AS A PURSUIT AND LIFESTYLE IS GOD'S WILL FOR YOU.

1 Thessalonians 4:3-5 teaches us:

> *It is God's will that you should be sanctified: that you should avoid sexual immorality; that each of you should learn to control your own body in a way that is holy and honorable, not in passionate lust like the pagans, who do not know God;* (NIV)

These verses answer the big "why" questions?

Why should I be concerned about staying away from sexual sin?

Why should I control my body and live in a way that honors God?

Paul clearly answers those questions in two ways.

First, it is God's will for us to be holy.

No follower of Christ needs to pray about what God's will is concerning sexual sin; He's already clearly revealed that.

The word "holy" means to be "set apart." No true victory will occur until you are "set apart" from sexual sin and "set apart" unto God, fully committing and yielding this area of your life to His control. His will is never burdensome or oppressive. On the contrary, obeying it brings genuine freedom.

These verses also give us a second answer to the "why" questions. The most important thing you can do in overcoming sin and in your pursuit of purity is get to know God. The Bible says that the difference between those who are controlled by sexual sin and those who know how to control their own body in holiness and honor is the difference between those who know God and those who do not.

Knowing God is indispensable to overcoming sexual sin because when you know God you come to see His purity, His pardon for your sin, and His power to change you. May God imbed these "why" answers deeply in your heart so you live out His will as a lifestyle.

If you are going to overcome sexual sin and walk in the freedom God offers, the third truth that is vital for you to understand is that:

GOD HAS GIVEN YOU THE POWER OF THE SPIRIT AND THE FREEDOM TO CHOOSE TO CONTINUALLY TAKE THE "WAY OF ESCAPE".

In your battle for sexual purity, you can be assured of an awesome promise:

> *No temptation has overtaken you except what is common to mankind. And God is faithful; he will not let you be tempted beyond what you can bear. But when you are tempted, he will also provide a way out so that you can endure it.* (1 Corinthians 10:13, NIV)

Your temptations are common! You are not alone. God promises that because of His faithfulness, there is ALWAYS a way of escape!

An undeniable but simple truth about temptation is that it

wouldn't be a temptation if it wasn't tempting. Sex outside of God's boundaries wouldn't be tempting if it wasn't attractive and pleasurable, for the short term. The Bible states: "there is a passing, or fleeting pleasure in sin" (Hebrews 11:25) but it's always short-lived pleasure, but with painful long-term consequences.

If you are going to escape sexual sin and walk in the freedom God offers, you have to know Him first.

The fourth and final vital truth is that:

VICTORY OVER SEXUAL SIN REQUIRES A MUTUAL PARTNERSHIP BETWEEN YOU AND GOD.

God will not do what He has given you the ability to do, and you cannot do God's part.

The truth of partnership is seen throughout Scripture. 1 Corinthians 10:13 says that when we face temptation, God is faithful and will provide a way of escape so we can stand up under it. Our responsibility in this partnership is to take the way of escape.

Nehemiah 4:9 expresses this partnership between God and us as Nehemiah faced great danger from enemies who were opposing the rebuilding of the wall around Jerusalem. He said in response to their threats:

> *But we prayed to our God and posted a guard day and night to meet this threat.* (NIV)

They were in a distinct partnership with God – they cried out to God for His help and strength, yet they did their part in posting guards to protect the city.

Romans 8:13 also speaks of this partnership and gives a key truth to overcoming the desires of our sinful nature. It says:

> *...if by the Spirit you put to death the misdeeds of the body, you will live.* (NIV)

It's only through the Holy Spirit's help that we can consistently overcome sin and walk in freedom. If our own willpower alone was sufficient to walk in victory, many would already be walking in freedom. It's only by the Spirit that can we put to death the misdeeds of the body.

We've looked at a number of truths which require steps on our part to partner with God. Here are some final, but important, action steps He's given us to act on in overcoming sexual sin.

1. REPENT AND STOP

To genuinely repent means you turn from your sin. You turn to God, and you begin to live differently. No matter how great the challenge, the journey of a thousand miles begins with a single step.

2. GET SUPPORT

Having at least one person you trust and can reveal the darkest sides of yourself but still be loved unconditionally, is crucial. A biblical pattern is "Confession = Healing Power." When you are accountable and confess your sins to another, you invite others to help you in prayer and support. As you bring your sin out from under the cover of darkness and shine light upon it, much of its power is diffused.

3. CREATE A VICTORIOUS ENVIRONMENT

Having a self-awareness of things that trigger unwanted sexual behavior is key. A trigger is anything sexual, environmental or emotional in nature that causes you to want to engage in your unwanted sexual behavior. Four triggers are common enough to have their own acronym: H.A.L.T. (hungry, angry, lonely or tired).

4. PLAN AHEAD TO TAKE THE WAY OF ESCAPE

For every sexual trigger, develop a remedy action (whatever step you need to take to avoid your triggers).

5. CREATE AN ESCAPE PLAN

Retrain your heart and mind through memorizing Scripture.

Rehearse the devastating costs of sexual sin. Put your accountability partner in your phone's "Favorites" list. Focus on the "Yes" of coming to know God and seeing His purity, His pardon for your sin, and His power to change you.

May God help you to fully embrace this divine partnership. Know that as you do your part, the Holy Spirit will be faithful to empower and transform you.

I applaud you for reading this and encourage you to follow through on the action steps mentioned in this chapter. As you do, you will find a new freedom in Christ, an understanding of yourself, and what it takes to dump the worthless stuff from your life so you can experience God's best.

May you be able to walk with your head held high or lay your head down on a pillow for restful sleep because there is nothing to hide, nothing to be ashamed of, nothing to regret.

BIG IDEA:

Demolishing sexual sin is critical to constructing your life upon the Solid Rock.

GROUP STUDY QUESTIONS:

1. What are some specific consequences of sexual sin (for singles and/ or married)? How is the pain, shame and brokenness that comes from sexual sin understated in our culture? How is the joy and delight of following God's design for our sexuality understated?

2. What are some sexual triggers that you (or "people" – safer in a group context) are susceptible to? When are you (people) most vulnerable to sexual temptation?

3. What are several remedy actions or "ways of escape" you will utilize when you become aware you're being tempted?

4. Why is having an accountability partner important?

5. What are the two most important questions you'd advise an accountability partner to ask you when you meet?

6. What caused you to tell someone about your struggle with sexual sin? Who did you tell? Why did you go to them?

7. What is our role in partnership with the power of the Holy Spirit to gain freedom and transformation? What is the Holy Spirit's role in partnership with us to gain freedom and transformation?

8. What can you and your church do to help shed light on the issue of overcoming sexual sin?

9. After reading this chapter, what is one thing you will put into practice or one thing you will change in your life?

10. How can we, as a group, help you do this?

SECTION 2:

Building On A

Firm Foundation

-6-

METAMORPHOO:

TRANSFORMED BY GOD'S WORD

By Scott Kramer

Eggs. Bacon. Pancakes. Maple Syrup. These are a few of my favorite things.

Additionally, they are my favorite things in my favorite meal of the day: breakfast. In fact, if I would list my favorite breakfast, it would look something like this: a three-egg omelet with ham, bacon, peppers and cheddar cheese, 2 pancakes on the side swimming in maple syrup (maybe even drowning), and very dark roast coffee on the side, black. Very dark roast. Have your salivary glands started to react yet to those mental images? Mine sure have.

So many men, just like me, have a very clear picture of the kinds of foods they love to eat! They know their favorite restaurants, their favorite desserts, and even their favorite coffee blends (Starbucks Sumatra for me). We are rarely hesitant to invest time, money and energy into feeding our bodily appetites, and feeding them well.

Yet, I wonder how much energy we are investing in feeding our spiritual appetite. Most of us eat two, three, or even four meals a day to nourish our physical man, yet at the same time we unwittingly fail to nourish our inner man. In the words of the biblical author James, *"My brothers, this should not be."* (James 3:10, NIV)

This pattern of nourishment and malnourishment (physically and spiritually) described above was also the pattern of my life until my junior year in college. I grew up going to church in Berks County, PA. After graduating high school, I went to Emory University in Atlanta, GA to study biology and pre-med.

On arrival, with the newfound freedom that most new college students feel, church attendance and Bible reading were not high on the priority list. I was still a follower of Christ. I would never have denied my Christian roots and belief in Christ as the Son of God, but I wasn't living a thriving and victorious life as a believer. This is the way it goes for many young men who grow up in church and go off to a secular university. It was no different for me. That is, of course, until I met Carl.

More unique and unusual men certainly must exist, but Carl would rank highly among them. Typically clad in worn out jeans, an old windbreaker jacket with his name on the left side, and generally uncombed hair, Carl sauntered into my life. Carl had a very unique way about him, and a very unique calling.

When I was in college in the mid-90s, Carl had a deep burden to evangelize and disciple college baseball players in the Atlanta area. Pretty unusual, right? In fact, his calling was so clear that he had constructed batting cages in his backyard so that he could invite college baseball players over for free batting practice, along with a free introduction to Jesus.

Carl impacted many young men for Jesus. I am one of them.

As I said earlier, he quite literally sauntered into my life. No, really, he had a walking gait that couldn't be described in any other way than a saunter. One day my friend, Artie, our first basemen on the Emory baseball team, invited me and my twin brother, Jeff, to join him in his dorm room for a Bible study that would be led by this guy named Carl.

I refused the invitation several times because I 'didn't have time.' Eventually, though, I found myself sitting in the dorm room with my twin brother, Artie, two other baseball friends, and Carl.

Probably for the first several weeks, or maybe even months, I sat there nodding and smiling, trying to pretend that I understood even half of what Carl was talking about, and all the while he talked 20,000 feet over my head about the Bible. Can you relate??

One might have said that if you just hang around with him long enough, eventually it's got to rub off on you, right? Well, I'm happy to report that in this case, osmosis did its work. After months of attending, as Carl would talk about faith, about covenants, about the cross, and about the Bible, osmosis began to take effect. The truths of God's Word began to penetrate my spirit by way of my mind and my heart.

Part of this truth permeation that was most successful was my memorization of what I still believe to be one of the most important verses in the Bible.

Hebrews 4:12 tells us this:

> *For the word of God is alive and active. Sharper than any double-edged sword, it penetrates even to dividing soul and spirit, joints and marrow; it judges the thoughts and attitudes of the heart. (NIV)*

In the 1984 NIV, (the version I was reading at the time) I remember the first part reading this way: *"For the word of God is living and active."*

This was one of Carl's favorites, and thus became one of mine. This inspired verse establishes for us the eternal truth that God's Word is living and active. God's Word is alive and at work!!

Aside from the usual John 3:16 that all self-respecting, born and raised in the church Christians typically know, Heb. 4:12 became the first verse to be permanently etched on my heart. I didn't know then that two decades later, this verse would still be lodged deep within my spirit, still producing fruit in my life.

You see, that's one of the unmistakable by-products of having God's Word planted in your heart. It produces fruit.

God's Word has an unchangeable nature of being described as a seed that is living and active. When it finds fertile soil in the heart of a follower of Christ, it takes root.

In 1993, Carl knew what I didn't. He knew that when God's Word finds a place in your heart, it produces a harvest of righteousness in your life. I'm forever grateful to Carl for the seeds of truth he planted in my life. He trained me on how to nourish my spirit man on God's Word every day (at that time, it was typically over a bowl of Fruity Pebbles), and I am forever changed.

So why am I telling you this story? Some of you have already learned the power of storing God's Word in your heart. But many of you haven't. Let me share with you another biblical reason illustrating the importance of a daily habit in God's Word.

Here it is: Romans: 12:2:

> *Do not conform to the pattern of this world, but be transformed by the renewing of your mind. Then you will be able to test and approve what God's will is—his good, pleasing and perfect will.* (NIV)

Paul's words here in the book of Romans are not only the second Bible verse I committed to permanent memory; they also not-so-cryptically articulate the secret to life change.

Let me explain. Here in chapter 12 of the letter to the believers in Rome, Paul tells us a not-so-secret secret. I call it a secret because I meet so few people who understand it, yet it's written for us in plain vanilla. Under the inspiration of the Holy Spirit, Paul reveals to us the pathway to being changed: renewing your mind.

He literally says *'be transformed by the renewing of your mind.'*

The importance of this verse cannot be overstated. The word that is translated in English to "transformed", is the Greek word "*metamorphoo*".

This Greek word, as defined by James Strong, literally means "*to change into another form.*"[1] In a world where our minds are inundated daily with the patterns of this world (music, movies, vulgarity at work, suggestive images, etc), the gravity of having our minds renewed daily with God's Word is paramount.

The unique aspect of this transformation that often eludes us is the fact that there's only one person who can initiate this daily mind renewal in your life. And that person is YOU.

Only you can cultivate the right disciplines in your life that facilitate daily growth. Nobody else can do this for you. Nobody!

In fact, not even God can do this for you!! Friend, learning how to establish a daily Bible reading habit in your life may be the single most important habit you ever aim to create. There are few other daily habits that possess an equal potential to produce transformation in your life!!

Allow me to share with you how this looks in my life. It hasn't changed much, actually. While I don't eat Fruity Pebbles anymore (I'm forty-two, and I don't think they make it anymore), I still read God's Word every day for 5-10 minutes over breakfast.

Now some of you are thinking "That's not enough!" Well, you are right, and you are wrong.

You are right in that if that is all the time I ever spent in God's Word, then it probably would not be sufficient for me to truly become a man of the Word. (I have attended & led small group Bible studies for 2 decades. That completes the diet!)

But, you are wrong in that 5-10 minutes a day IS adequate time for God's Word to be strategically planted regularly in your heart to produce a harvest of righteousness.

Here's why: Transformation isn't a microwave, it's a crock pot.

Don't think in terms of sprinting, but rather in terms of running a marathon!

Let's do the math. 10 minutes a day times 365 days a year gives you 3,650 minutes in God's Word every year.

Every 5 years that's 18,250 minutes.

Every 10 years, you have 36,500 minutes in God's Word. That's a lot of seed planting!!

Remember, the Psalmist writes in 119:11:

> *I have hidden your word in my heart that I might not sin against you.* (NIV)

When you commit to this daily hiding of God's Word, transformation is around the corner.

If we, as men, are going to become the leaders in our homes, workplaces and communities that God is calling us to be, then we need to establish strong habits in our daily routines.

---Habits that posture our inner man to be strong and transformed.

---Habits that create a resistance to sin in our lives.

---Habits that renew our minds and transform our spirits.

---Habits that centralize the importance and the power of God's Word in our lives.

---Habits that afford us the daily opportunity to nourish our inner man on the bread of life.

---Habits like the one I have had for over twenty years now, that has changed my life forever.

So men, let's get started! As in, right away!

Tomorrow morning, block out 10 minutes to spend in God's Word.

Start marking your Bible, underlining things that impact you, and track what you've read with simple numbers or letters after each chapter you read.

I do this so I know how many times I've read each book.

Over the long haul, you'll start to see the power in this! And very quickly, you will start to notice the metamorphoo taking place in your life.

So start tomorrow. Wake up 10 minutes earlier, find your spot, and start building your habit!!

BIG IDEA:

We are called to renew our minds. This is done through the reading of God's Word. There's only one person who can initiate this daily mind renewal in your life.

Only you can cultivate the right disciplines in your life that facilitate daily growth. Nobody else can do this for you. So start tomorrow. Wake up 10 minutes earlier, find your spot, and start building your habit!!

GROUP STUDY QUESTIONS:

1. Why is it important to renew our minds?

2. Why is the Bible key to our mind renewal?

3. The author said, "Transformation isn't a microwave, it's a crockpot." What does this mean?

4. How often do you read the Bible?

5. What keeps you from spending time in the Bible?

6. How can you be more intentional in your Bible reading time?

7. After reading this chapter, what is one thing you will put into practice or one thing you will change in your life?

8. How can we, as a group, help you do this?

THE FOUNDATION OF PRAYER

By: John Bowman

I lead a small group of twelve men that meet Sunday night in my basement. We discuss various topics on what it means to be a godly man, husband and father.

One Sunday night I posed a question to the men. I asked them to rate themselves on a scale of 1-10 on their level of spiritual leadership in the home (1 being poor, 10 being excellent).

As we went around the room, the answers varied between five and eight.

Next, I asked them to rate the level of their devotional life with God, time spent in prayer and bible reading, using the same grading format.

Again, we went around the room and the numbers given did not match up with the numbers given for the spiritual leader. In fact, some of the numbers given for their devotional life were lower than the numbers given as the spiritual leader.

As I sat there, the following statement came to my mind:

"A spiritual leader is a godly leader. A godly leader is a godly man; and a godly man is a man that is devoted to God."

So, the question is: "How can we be a spiritual leader in our families if we are not first a man devoted to God?"

Spending time with God is vital to our very lives, whether it is five minutes or one hour. The key to spending time with God is to discipline ourselves daily to spending time in prayer.

It may start slow, and you may sometimes forget. But just like an athlete, be disciplined.

Living a life of devotion will not happen without discipline.

The reason many men never have an effective devotional life is that they never plan for it.

They do not know what it is because they have never taken the time to find out.

They do not pray because they do not set aside the time.

Their character never rises to that of Christ's because they do not expose their lives to His pure light.

In this chapter, we are going to look at some obstacles and solutions that will help men in their personal prayer and devotions to the Lord.

HOW OFTEN DO WE PRAY?

I'm not talking about a prayer said before a meal, bedtime or throughout the day. Don't get me wrong, all these prayers are good. However, I'm asking how often do we, as men, sit down and spend an intentional time with the Lord in prayer and devotions?

Why is it so difficult for men to have prayer and devotions?

What are some obstacles that keep men from praying and having devotions?

PERSONAL DEVOTIONS TAKE DISCIPLINE

All athletes are disciplined in their training. Athletes train their bodies to win a prize that will fade away, but as Christians we train the spirit man for an eternal prize.

1 Corinthians 9:25 says:

> *Everyone who competes in the games goes into strict training. They do it to get a crown that will not last, but we do it to get a crown that will last forever.* (NIV)

Have you ever started a workout regiment?

I remember at twelve years old my foster dad, Homer, taught my brother and I how to lift weights. As a pre-teen while I was power lifting weights in the driveway, my friends were riding bikes and hanging out. It was hard, knowing that I could be having fun with my friends, but I liked the fact that I was relatively stronger than most boys my age.

I continued to work out into my adult life. I even achieved bench-pressing over 300 pounds!

Now do you think that I was able to achieve this feat after just one day of lifting weights? NO!

It took hours and hours of discipline.

Not just physical discipline, but mental discipline.

I was thirty-eight years old when I ran my first 5k. I hated running! For me, it was a punishment.

Did I wake up one day and run a 5k?

NO! It started with walking 1 mile and then 2 miles and slowly I increased to jogging and then running.

I think about this whenever I go to the gym or workout at the park.

You know what the hardest part is? Doing it! Profound, huh?

The hardest part is making the time to get in the car and go. But each time I would feel good, and I would want to go again.

Can I say that I have always been faithful?

No! It's a struggle.

But I know the more I go, the more I will want to go. I will begin to see results, and I will feel healthy. The doctor will be happy! My wife will be happy! My kids and grandkids will be happy! I will be happy! Get the picture?

Now, let's take that same principle and apply it to our spiritual life. Look at 1 Timothy 4:8:

> *For physical training is of some value, but godliness has value for all things, holding promise for both the present life and the life to come.* (NIV)

Three years ago I read a book called "My One Word," by Mike Ashcraft and Rachel Olsen.

"The concept of My One Word is simple. Lose the long list of resolutions—all your sweeping promises to change—and do something about one thing this year instead of nothing about everything. Choose just one word that represents what you most hope God will do in you, and focus on it for an entire year."[1]

This book helped me begin to examine my life, both physical and spiritual. I had always prayed, but it was haphazard. Being a very busy man, I needed to structure my prayer life.

I started with the word "discipline." (Sound familiar?)

Then the second year I needed to increase my "discipline" and so I went with the word "determined." I was "determined" to be "disciplined!"

This year I believe the Lord wanted me to go to another level so my one word is "intentional."

OBSTACLES THAT KEEP MEN FROM PRAYER/DEVOTIONS

1. I'm too busy

Let's be real, most men work long hours each day. However, how important is God to you? How about your friendship with God?

> *Teach us to number our days, that we may gain a heart of wisdom.* (Psalm 90:12, NIV)

Let the Author of time show you how to manage your time. Remember it's not the quantity, but the quality. Start with 5 minutes and see where that goes.

2. I don't know how to pray

The disciples asked Jesus: *"Lord, teach us to pray"* (Luke 11:1, NIV)

A simple way to pray is by using this acronym: A.C.T.S.

Adore

I like to open my time with God with a worship song that helps me to center my thoughts on God and bring me into His presence. I personally like "Have It All" by Bethel, a perfect prayer song.

Confess

Ask God to forgive you of sins that you know of, but also sins you do not know of.

> *Search me, God, and know my heart; test me and know my anxious thoughts. See if there is any offensive way in me, and lead me in the way everlasting.* (Psalm 139:23-24, NIV)

Confessing is simply admitting to God that we have sinned and we need Him.

Thankfulness

There are so many things we can thank God for. Health, provisions, job, family etc. I like sitting in my living room and looking at the pictures of my wife, my sons and their wives, and our five grandchildren and thanking God for them.

Supplication

The definition of supplication is *"the action of asking or begging for something earnestly or humbly."*

I think in today's world, we have a lot to pray for and about.

Look around! Not only can we pray for others, but we can also pray for ourselves. Remember, God cares for you!

> *Be anxious for nothing, but in everything by prayer and supplication with thanksgiving let your requests be made known to God.* (Philippians 4:6, NIV)

Sometimes we ask: "Why should I pray? God already knows what I'm going to say."

Yes, God does know what we are going to say before we say it. In fact, He even knows before we think it! When we verbally pray to God, it is telling Him that we are dependent on Him instead of ourselves to meet a need that may be in our life.

3. There are too Many Distractions

> *But Jesus often withdrew to lonely places and prayed.* (Luke 5:16, NIV)

It could be at the park, in your car, your bedroom, your man cave---wherever you can spend the time. I use my office at home in the morning to spend time with God.

When we gave our lives to Christ, the Holy Spirit began to make His dwelling in us. The Word of God says we were like infants:

> *Then we will no longer be infants, tossed back and forth by the waves, and blown here and there by every wind of teaching and*

by the cunning and craftiness of people in their deceitful scheming. (Ephesians 4:14, NIV)

To grow into a mature godly man, the spirit man in us needs to grow. One of the ways to grow into a godly man is by having a prayer/devotional life.

Galatians 5:17 says:

For the flesh desires what is contrary to the Spirit, and the Spirit what is contrary to the flesh. They are in conflict with each other, so that you are not to do whatever you want. (NIV)

Each of them wants to grow and have control.

A scripture that I often pray, in fact it's the scripture that drives my life, is Psalm 40:8:

I desire to do your will, my God; (NIV)

Now because of my intentional prayer/devotional life, the first thought that comes to my mind in the morning is spending time with God.

What about you? Is it your desire to grow in the Lord?

If so, an intentional prayer and devotion life is necessary.

The title of this book is "Under Construction" and you know the most important part of a home is the foundation. Prayer/devotions are essential to laying a spiritual foundation and helping us to develop ourselves into godly men.

The question for prayerless men is a very masculine one. It comes from the book, "The Disciplines of a Godly Man," by Kent Hughes:

"Are we man enough to meditate? To confess? To adore? To submit? To sweat and endure?"[2]

The key is "intentionality."

Start today to begin an intentional prayer/devotional life with God and build your spiritual foundation in Him.

Set aside time each day.

Find a quiet place…if none exists, create one.

Then just talk to God

One final thought from God's Word:

> *I looked for someone among them who would build up the wall and stand before me in the gap on behalf of the land so I would not have to destroy it, but I found no one.* (Ezekiel 22:30, NIV)

God is searching for faithful men. He is searching for men He can trust to intercede on behalf of our nation. God is looking for men He can trust with God-sized tasks.

Will you be that man?

Will His eyes rest on you or pass over you?

When it comes to prayer and devotions, it's like Nike says, "Just Do It!"

BIG IDEA:

"A spiritual leader is a godly leader. A godly leader is a godly man and a godly man is a man that is devoted to God."

We show our devotion by intentionally spending time with God in prayer. A solid prayer life is a key to developing a solid foundation in our spiritual life.

GROUP STUDY QUESTIONS:

1. Rate yourself on a scale of 1-10 on your level of spiritual leadership in the home---1 being poor 10 being excellent.

2. Rate your level of spiritual devotions to God using the same grading format.

3. How often do you pray?

4. What keeps you from spending time in prayer?

5. How can you be more intentional in your prayer time?

6. After reading this chapter, what is one thing you will put into practice or one thing you will change in your life?

7. How can we, as a group, help you do this?

8

SANCTIFICATION

By: Jim Leake

What is sanctification?

It's not a word used frequently in today's culture. Let's explore together what sanctification is and what it is not.

Sanctification means *"to construct a life set apart for an exclusive purpose."*

I grew up on a farm in Western Maryland. Our home was filled with the aroma of freshly baked bread on a daily basis. The first thing my mother did as she prepared to bake the bread was retrieve the pan that was used exclusively for mixing bread dough. She didn't use this pan to wash dishes or clean vegetables. It was sanctified for the purpose of baking bread.

As a pastor I stood before many excited couples and led them in marriage vows. Those vows were a statement of sanctification. Each of them declared their exclusive dedication to one another.

One of the practices in the church is the dedication of newborns. Often parents choose a Scripture which states their desire for that child. Wise parents are declaring their desire for their child to fulfill

God's purpose.

This practice dates back to the Old Testament. 1 Samuel tells the story of Hannah. Hannah was so desperate to have a son that she made a promise to God. If God answered her prayer and gave her a son, she would dedicate her son totally to serve God.

This was a lofty desire of Hannah, but it was necessary for Samuel to agree and apply himself for this purpose. The result was Samuel accepted this challenge and became God's answer to a nation that was far from God. Samuel made his own personal choice to live a life set apart to God...to be sanctified.

The Old Testament also tells us a sad story of Samson. His parents chose to dedicate him to fulfill the purpose of God. God needed a man who would build the nation of Israel into a powerful force, leading them in victory over the warring nations that were oppressing them. Samson grew and chose to defy God's plan and satisfy sinful desires. His life ended in tragedy.

We all can tell stories about friends who attended church with their families when we were young. Their parents stood with other parents in a dedication service and lifted the newborn in prayer. They were sincere in their desire. They wanted that child to fulfill God's purpose. However, each of us must make a decision to build our lives on a relationship with Christ.

My life was greatly impacted by an incident in my young life. I was brought to church by my parents as a teenager. I sat in the last row with a close friend. His parents brought him on that same Sunday night.

The evangelist preached and gave an invitation for dedication. I turned to my friend and asked if he would join me at the altar. His reply was, "Jim, I will sometime, but not tonight. I have some things I want to do."

I went to the altar. He went out the back door. He joined with friends who were partying. They decided to get in a car and drive to another location. The police saw them run through a red light and started following the car. Instead of stopping, they began to speed.

As they drove around a bend, the driver lost control of the car. The car turned over, and my friend fell out. The car door came across his head, and he was rushed to the hospital in critical condition.

The doctors saved the life of my friend, but he was no longer the young man I knew. After months of rehabilitation, he was sent to an Adult Group Home. This happened over 50 years ago. My friend never held a job, never married, never fathered a child and never talked again. I saw him recently, and while he knew me, we couldn't converse.

Why do I tell this story? We all need to make our own decision to construct our lives through sanctification for the purpose of becoming like Christ.

The Scriptures give us three building blocks to construct a sanctified life.

PROMPTLY

The moment we profess our faith in the death and resurrection of Jesus we begin building our spiritual life free from all sin and righteous in the sight of God. We start to be sanctified when we accept Christ into our lives. But it doesn't end there.

PROGRESSIVE

None of us lives a perfect life. We all struggle with wrong choices. As we build this walk with Christ, forgiveness is provided when we repent.

Our sanctification is progressive as we grow. Our daily goal is to act as Christ would act. Sanctification should take place throughout our entire life as we daily leave the world's ways behind and become more like Jesus.

PERFECT, PERMANENT

Our building a life dedicated to God ends by death or the rapture of the church.

God's purpose for us is our sanctification, living separate lives in purity. We are sanctified when we live according to God's purpose or design.

> *One final word, friends. We ask you—urge is more like it—that you keep on doing what we told you to do to please God, not in a dogged religious plod, but in a living, spirited dance. You know the guidelines we laid out for you from the Master Jesus. God wants you to live a pure life.*
>
> *Keep yourselves from sexual promiscuity.*
>
> *Learn to appreciate and give dignity to your body, not abusing it, as is so common among those who know nothing of God.* (1 Thessalonians 4:1-5, Message Bible)

This passage balances both the positive and the negative instructions for our journey to build a life dedicated to God.

Notice the considerable space the Holy Spirit designates for sexual purity. This message is extremely vital in the church today.

> *For this is the will of God, even your sanctification, that ye should abstain from fornication: That every one of you should know how to possess his vessel in sanctification and honor;* (1 Thessalonians 4:3-4, KJV).

Scripture calls us to reject the popular view of the world around us, especially when it comes to sex and marriage and purity. However, sanctification has both positive and negative features. We need to be set apart to God and separate from sin.

> *Don't suppress the Spirit, and don't stifle those who have a word from the Master. On the other hand, don't be gullible. Check out everything, and keep only what's good. Throw out anything tainted with evil.* (1 Thessalonians 5:19-22, Message Bible)

Like it or not, partial obedience means disobedience.

The Bible calls us to be holy.

The seriousness of the truth of sanctification is clearly stated by God:

Be Holy for I am Holy. (1 Peter 1:16, NIV)

Without holiness no man can see the LORD. (Hebrews 12:14, NIV)

How can any man live a sanctified life?

It is not possible unless we live a joint venture in cooperation with the Holy Spirit, with the Father and the promise of God's Word.

It is never too late. Though Samson chose to reject God's plan for his life, he realized he needed God; when he called on God, God answered his prayer. My friend was not able to enjoy many of life's most celebrated moments, but he has celebrated the acceptance and forgiveness of God.

We have answered the question, "What is sanctification?" Now let's discover what it is not.

Sanctification is not accomplished by conforming to a set of rules that apply to the outer man and referred to as external holiness.

Misguided teachers and misinterpreted Scripture do not add to or subtract from being set apart to God. This is a mistaken belief and is preached in some churches.

Jesus had the strongest rebuke for the religious rulers of His day known as the Pharisees who were rule keepers. They considered themselves to be righteous by how they dressed and how they kept religious observances. Jesus called them *"whitened grave stones full of dead men's bones."* (Matthew 23:27)

It would be difficult to calculate how many sincere seekers after God have been turned off and turned away by the expectations of having to conform to a standard which had little merit for their spiritual maturity. Often rule keepers enforced the adornment of the outer man and neglected the truth the Spirit revealed concerning the inner sanctified man.

May God himself, the God who makes everything holy and whole, make you holy and whole, put you together—spirit, soul, and body — and keep you fit for the coming of our

> *Master, Jesus Christ. The One who called you is completely dependable. If he said it, he'll do it!* (1 Thessalonians 5:23-24, Message Bible)

God and His Word are what guide us in our sanctification, not man-made rules. When we guide our lives after God's principles, we daily become more sanctified, waiting for the day when perfection comes through death or the rapture.

BIG IDEA:

Sanctification is the life-long process of becoming less like the world and more like Jesus. We are called to a lifetime of defeating sinful tendencies and replacing them with godly behavior practices. We are all called to become holy as Jesus was Holy. We can live a sanctified holy life.

GROUP STUDY QUESTIONS:

1. What does sanctification mean? How does it apply to you personally?

2. Is sanctification a one-time thing or a life-long act?

3. When is sanctification finished in our lives?

4. The author said, "Partial obedience means disobedience..." What does this mean?

5. How do we live a sanctified life?

6. What's the difference between sanctification and legalism?

7. After reading this chapter, what is one thing you will put into practice or one thing you will change in your life?

8. How can we, as a group, help you do this?

SINKING IN OUR SOUL

By: Tom Rees

My garage floor has sunk in spots by six inches. There are major cracks in each quadrant, and it looks like we have a costly repair ahead of us because a proper base wasn't put in when the house was built.

The Master Builder recognizes the dangers of what happens to our lives when we cut corners and fail to put in the proper base.

Sabbath, spiritual rest, is the rebar that gives strength to our soul, that helps us to hold up in the storms that bombard our lives.

It is one of the Ten Commandments:

Remember the Sabbath day by keeping it holy. (Exodus 20:8, NIV)

Yet, it is the one that many Christ followers, including those in leadership, ignore the most.

When we fail to honor the Sabbath, here are some of the sinkholes that form in our lives in the area of rest/work balance:

NEGATIVITY

We see everything from a glass-half-empty perspective. We judge others harshly and see interactions with others from the worst possible perspective. It can become an "us against the world" mentality.

ANGER

We have a short fuse and can blow up quickly over little things. People may be afraid to approach us because we make mountains out of molehills. So instead, people feel like they are walking on eggshells around us. Unfortunately, those that are closest to us, sustain the most collateral damage from our anger.

TENSION

We can become bossy and rigid as a leader. The tension spreads and communication tends to be curt, abrupt, and snappy. There is no joy in our lives and people no longer enjoy being around us.

ESCAPISM

We want to feel alive again so we escape into a fantasy that makes us feel good, successful and valued. This can lead to pornography, affairs, alcoholism and drug addiction that destroy us from the inside out.

STAGNATION

We find ourselves stuck. Fatigue sets in, and we struggle to get work done. It is like walking in quicksand, and the more we try to move forward, the more stuck we feel. Tunnel vision can set in, and we can find ourselves zapped of creativity and vision.

ADRENALINE

It is hard for some of us to settle our souls and rest because we are addicted to adrenaline. The adrenaline rush feels great when we are attacking a problem or completing a big project, but we can get addicted to it. Over the long haul, it can turn on us and destroy us. Our bodies were not built to constantly live off the fuel of adrenaline.

SICKNESS

We try to cheat our biological response to fast food, junk food and lack of sleep by using energy drinks and double shot lattes. Eventually, our poor health habits catch up to us with diabetes, cardiac failure and/or chronic recurring illnesses.

THE NEED FOR SABBATH

Probably in a hope to influence my behavior in a positive way, Courtney, my oldest daughter, gave me the classic "The Sabbath" by Jewish theologian Abraham Joshua Heschel. He speaks of how, on the seventh day, God gave the world a soul. For us, it renews our soul and helps us to rediscover who we are.

It has been one of the most inspirational books I have read. Heschel writes that the Sabbath is:

"a mine where spirit's precious metal can be found"[1]

"a day that ennobles the soul and makes the body wise"[2]

"not a date but an atmosphere"[3]

Wayne Muller, author of "Sabbath: Finding Rest, Renewal, and Delight in Our Busy Lives," challenges us with the importance of Sabbath when he writes, "Like a path through the forest, Sabbath creates a marker for ourselves so, if we are lost, we can find our way back to our center."[4]

We can find ourselves lost in our own success. The Master Builder laid out the plans for us to work and subdue the world around us for six days and then take a day of rest. Yet our very success in the subdue and take dominion aspects can cause us to think, "If I work and am rewarded for six days of good work, then seven days straight will reward me with even more benefits." The reality is that our body, mind and soul begin to suffer, and we become less effective like the logger that chops down trees without taking time to sharpen his axe.

DEVELOPING AN ACTION PLAN

As I get estimates to repair my garage floor, I have been presented with three options:

Option One is to hire a company that does mudjacking. They come in and drill holes in the concrete floor and then pump in pulverized stone, effectively pushing it up from below.

Option Two is to pull out the garage floor, get the foundation right and then put in a new floor.

Option Three is to pretend there is no problem with the foundation. Pour a new floor. Sell the house and move!

Often we choose the option that fixes the cosmetic problem but do not get to the root of the problem, and further cracks and sinkholes occur. We have to commit to getting the foundation right.

In his book "Rooted," Banning Liebscher issues this prophetic warning for ministry leaders, "If you love the spotlight more than the secret place, you're in trouble, because it means you care more about pleasing people than pleasing God."[5]

Several years ago, I took a Zero Risk assessment. When I met with my coach to discuss the assessment, my friend and coach made this observation, "Tom, you are highly loyal and dedicated to the organizations that you work for and will sacrifice yourself for the ministry, including your health and family."

Ouch! That began a journey where I had to find my way back to center. Here are some things I have done to become more intentional in this area to get healthier and more whole:

Take Time with God.

The trap that many men fall into is trying to navigate life on our own without taking daily time with God. I felt I needed time with God to talk about our relationship and the issues and responsibilities of my life as a husband, father and man of God.

> *He makes me lie down in green pastures, He leads me beside quiet waters, He refreshes my soul. He guides me along the right paths for His name's sake."* (Psalm 23: 2,3, NIV)

ACTION: When do you take daily time with God?

_____

_____

_____

Do Something Different.

Since my job is normally inside at a desk or around conference tables, I take time on my Sabbath to do something outdoors and active. Biking and hiking are great ways to get out and enjoy what God has created. "Resting" on the Sabbath may mean something totally different for a landscaper or contractor. The importance is to switch from what your normal weekly rhythm is to something that brings a healthy contrast.

ACTION: Where do you go on your Sabbath?

What are the things that replenish your body and soul?

_____

_____

_____

Reprioritize your Life.

Richard Swenson in "The Overload Syndrome" states that "overload is what we do when we forget who God is."[6]

Several years ago, I made some changes to address overload in my life. I was burning the candle at both ends, and it was showing up in my health. My emotional and spiritual gauges were showing that I was running on fumes. To regain control of my schedule I pulled back from most of my lower-tier commitments. God, family, work and serving held the top tiers, but I let go of fantasy football, cable television and multiple volunteer committees that created death by meetings.

Again, our success can create more work that can ultimately cause us to lose the edge that helped us become successful in the first place.

ACTION: What are some things you need to off load so that you can get back to Sabbath and balance in your life?

_____

_____

_____

Take a Sabbatical.

To recalibrate, I took some extended time off. I felt that one day wasn't going to fix my depleted state. There is something healthy that comes from taking extended time to recalibrate.

In Exodus 23:10-11, God instructed His chosen people, *"Plant and harvest your crops for six years, but let the land be renewed and lie uncultivated during the seventh year."* (NLT)

There are times we need to do this with our lives as well.

Also, be careful that all your vacation time doesn't become extended work project time. If it takes you a few days to detox from work, build in bumper time on the front end as well as the tail end of vacation. This cushion can help you to not get sidetracked by the thoughts of all you need to do when you get back. My best vacations have been when I have put two weeks back to back.

ACTION: When can you plan on taking some extended time to recalibrate your life?

_____

_____

Journal.

Technology has many advantages, but I prefer to carry a notebook that serves as my journal and action book.

As I take time to hear from God, I can write it down so I do not forget. Also, it allows me to focus prayerfully and strategically on my 6 x 6 Goals.

At the Willow Creek Leadership Summit a few years back, I heard Bill Hybels talk about putting bursts of energy into his goals.

I have taken this wisdom, and several times a year I will take an extended meditative time to process 6 things I will work on for the next 6 weeks.

ACTION: What are your 6 x 6 Goals for the next six weeks?

1. _____
_____

2. _____
_____

3. _____
_____

4. _____
_____

5. _____
_____

6. _____
_____

BIG IDEA:

God laid out the plans for us to work and subdue the world around us for six days, and then take a day of rest. Avoiding this command causes our body, mind and soul to begin to suffer. We become less effective like the logger that chops down trees without taking time to sharpen his axe.

GROUP STUDY QUESTIONS:

1. Do you practice taking a Sabbath?

2. Why do people see this command as optional?

3. Which "sinkhole" develops in you when you neglect a Sabbath?

4. What do you already do or can begin doing on your Sabbath?

5. What can you stop doing in your life to allow you to take a Sabbath?

6. After reading this chapter, what are 6 things you will work on for the next 6 weeks?

7. How can we, as a group, help you do this?

SECTION 3: Framing: Building Godly Character

SUFFERING THROUGH THE STORMS

By: Wayne Schaffer

Paul is an excellent example of a man who lived his calling amidst suffering. During his travels he relied on the Holy Spirit to tell him when to stay and when to leave. When prompted to leave Tyre he was led to Caesarea where he stayed with Philip the evangelist.

> *After we had been there a number of days, a prophet named Agabus came down from Judea. Coming over to us, he took Paul's belt, tied his own hands and feet with it and said, "The Holy Spirit says, 'In this way the Jewish leaders in Jerusalem will bind the owner of this belt and will hand him over to the Gentiles.'"*
>
> *When we heard this, we and the people there pleaded with Paul not to go up to Jerusalem. Then Paul answered, "Why are you weeping and breaking my heart? I am ready not only to be bound, but also to die in Jerusalem for the name of the Lord Jesus."* (Acts 21:10-13, NIV)

Paul was given a glimpse into his future and would not be swayed. This is a man unafraid to live the call on his life. He continues his trial-filled journey, encountering interrogation and imprisonment, not for anything he did, but simply for having hope.

Paul is soon arrested and put on a ship bound for Rome with other prisoners. Brutal winds accompany a storm making it impossible to travel, when Paul speaks up,

> *"Men, I can see that our voyage is going to be disastrous and bring great loss to ship and cargo, and to our own lives also."*
>
> *But the centurion, instead of listening to what Paul said, followed the advice of the pilot and of the owner of the ship. Since the harbor was unsuitable to winter in, the majority decided that we should sail on, hoping to reach Phoenix and winter there. This was a harbor in Crete, facing both southwest and northwest.* (Acts 27:10-12, NIV)

Paul had forewarned the centurion that there would be trouble ahead. Instead of listening to Paul, who had been told by prophets what was going to happen, they ignore his warning and instead heeded the advice of the professionals. Their intentions were good. Crete had a reputation for being a safe harbor.

In 1993, Pennsylvania experienced one of the worst blizzards on record. Warning after warning went out to get home and stay home. Yet, the great adventurer that I am decided to drive 20 miles from State College to Bellefonte to pick up a friend.

I thought, "What could possibly go wrong? I have four-wheel drive, and everyone else will be off the road."

Well, what normally took forty minutes ended up taking several hours. Why? Because I had failed to heed the warnings of the impending storm.

Sometimes we think we can tough it out and make it to the other side simply because we are men, and nothing is going to get in our way. Yet those decisions can often times lead to destruction. We must constantly be attentive to the voice of the Holy Spirit.

When we are worshipping at church on Sunday morning, it's easy to make godly decisions. When we hear the sermon and let the Word sink in, it's still easy to make godly decisions. When we are out to lunch with our Christian friends, we are still able to make godly decisions, but what happens on Monday morning when we are alone? Are we able to make decisions based on godly principles and not out of good intentions?

We can't assume we know what's coming next in our lives. Instead, we need to pray daily and put our lives in the hands of our Creator. The sailors had the mind of the Lord on their boat, through Paul, but they refused to listen to Paul's wisdom. We have the mind of the Lord in our midst and need to be sure to consult Him in our decisions.

Too many Christians seek worldly advice for spiritual decisions. Even worse are those who surround themselves with people who only give what they want to hear.

There is a difference between godly encouragement and worldly suggestions. Surrounding yourself with coddlers will not help you grow in maturity in Christ. Seek fellowship and advice from seasoned men of God who have wisdom and experience on their side. Listening to someone who is living a life guided by the Holy Spirit is better than any advice you can gain elsewhere.

Pastor Mike Holt once said, "Sometimes our good intentions get in the way of how God wants to be intentionally good to us."

We need to be aware of what God wants.

Ask Him, "Lord, is this the decision where you are desiring to be intentionally good to me?"

God doesn't want to just be good to you. He doesn't hand out luck. He is a providential God whose desire is to provide for our needs.

As a father, I've always tried to plan fun things with my kids. Sometimes I hit it out of the park, but other times I'm met with whines of, "This is dumb," and "Do we have to do this?" Sometimes I'll get them involved in the planning process, letting them choose where to go and what to do. I am not a perfect dad, but I try to be intentionally good by authoring a good time.

Your heavenly Father is perfect, the Author and Perfecter of your faith, and He has pen-in-hand, authoring for you an intentionally good plan for your life. Sometimes He allows us to co-author with Him.

At times we can become anxious or confused when facing big decisions. When I was praying with my family about moving to pastor a new church, I came across part of a verse in Acts that said:

It seemed good to the Holy Spirit and to us. (Acts 15:28a, NIV)

When we include God in our decision-making, He will guide us by His Spirit and will make confidence out of what was once confusion.

As you move forward in life, don't hesitate to ask the Holy Spirit, "Does this seem good to You? Is this next step (job, move, relationship) right and good with Your plan for my life?"

Then listen and obey. The voice of the Holy Spirit sometimes comes as a whisper deep inside. Listen for the *yes, no,* or *not now* of God.

What we learn next from Paul is to never leave the gospel behind, no matter what journey we find ourselves on.

Paul found himself on a boat that was rocking, creaking, and about to be torn apart. He could have smugly said, "I told you so," as many of us do when we know we were right and wish they'd just listened to us.

> *As the storm turned into a hurricane the crew began tossing cargo overboard to lighten the load.*
>
> *When neither sun nor stars appeared for many days and the storm continued raging, we finally gave up all hope of being saved.*
>
> *After they had gone a long time without food, Paul stood up before them and said: "Men, you should have taken my advice not to sail from Crete; then you would have spared yourselves this damage and loss. But now I urge you to keep up your courage,*

because not one of you will be lost; only the ship will be destroyed. Last night an angel of the God to whom I belong and whom I serve stood beside me and said, 'Do not be afraid, Paul. You must stand trial before Caesar; and God has graciously given you the lives of all who sail with you.'

So keep up your courage, men, for I have faith in God that it will happen just as he told me. Nevertheless, we must run aground on some island." (Acts 27:20-26, NIV)

God never lost sight of Paul and even sent an angel to visit him on the ship in the middle of the storm, both to comfort him and to give him a message. God does the same for us. He is always watching and providing a way out of the storms of life.

We must look at the despairing world around us and remember that we are the ones sent to give the message of hope. We must tell the people around us, "God's hand will reach down and save you." We can do this boldly by the power given to us through the Holy Spirit.

When your co-worker comes to you with his marriage problems, instead of saying, "I'll pray for you," why not take a moment right then and say, "Do you mind if I pray with you now?" Let them know you believe in the power of the cross.

In the last days, things are going to get worse. We need to remember to bring our faith into the fearful situations coming our way and take advantage of the opportunities that we will have to share our faith with others. Biblical doctrine is already sinking around us. Everywhere we look we are confronted by a world falling to the lies of the enemy, yet we must remember to not only preach the cross, but to live our lives for Him at all times.

Always believe in a Jesus Who came to earth, died, and rose again and Who calls us to take up our crosses daily. We can't allow for our faith to be watered down, for the storms to threaten sinking our boats, by what the world deems acceptable. We must be aware and intentional with our faith, continuing to bring God into every situation we face.

Don't go to work and leave your faith behind.

Don't go to school and leave your faith behind.

Don't go to cultural events and leave your faith behind.

Don't go into the world and leave your faith behind.

Live your life as one who takes the cross into the middle of the crisis and offers an anchor of hope to those sinking around you. Bring your faith with you when in fearful situations. God is bigger than the situation, and you belong to Him.

The final thing we learn from this journey of Paul's is to allow the pieces of wood to become places of worship.

Paul instructed those aboard to not abandon the ship. We must not give up when life gets hard, we must not abandon the testimony in the making.

Just before dawn Paul urged them all to eat.

> *"For the last fourteen days," he said, "you have been in constant suspense and have gone without food—you haven't eaten anything. Now I urge you to take some food. You will need it to survive. Not one of you will lose a single hair from his head."*
>
> *After he said this he took some bread and gave thanks to God in front of them all. Then he broke it and began to eat. They were all encouraged and ate some food themselves.* (Acts 27:33-36, NIV)

The mission of God, the calling of Christ, faith lived out in the everyday, is bowing your head and praying in public before you eat your meal, but it is also worshipping in the midst of worry and publicly giving thanks to God in the middle of trials. Paul took a piece of bread and gave thanks to God in front of them all.

> *But the ship struck a sandbar and ran aground. The bow stuck fast and would not move, and the stern was broken to pieces by the pounding of the surf. The soldiers planned to kill the prisoners to prevent any of them from swimming away and escaping. But the centurion wanted to spare Paul's life and kept them from*

carrying out their plan. He ordered those who could swim to jump overboard first and get to land. The rest were to get there on planks or on other pieces of the ship. In this way everyone reached land safely. (Acts 27:41-44, NIV)

Some prisoners made it to dry land by floating on pieces of wood splintered apart from the ship. Perhaps Paul was one of them. I know if I were Paul, I would have taken a piece of wood as a souvenir. Imagine he took a small piece when he arrived safely on shore and tucked it into his pocket as a reminder. He could show it to people and say, "Look what God got us through, just as He said He would."

After all of this I'm thinking Paul was ready to relax. He's just survived a storm at sea and is safely back on land. He's probably wishing for some coffee and a quiet spot to reflect on everything that just happened.

Acts 28:3 goes on to say how he begins to collect wood for a fire when a viper appears and attaches itself to his hand. Paul has two choices, he can cower to the fear of the snakebite, which could be fatal, or choose to remember the piece of wood in his pocket, the reminder to have faith in fearful situations.

The natives watching make commentary that he must have done something wrong for this to happen. They assumed he was a murderer and that the sea goddess was having revenge.

We hear the same words when something happens in our lives, "He must have really messed up for that to happen."

Paul pays them no mind and simply shakes the snake off of his hand and into the fire. He suffers no ill effects from the bite. Paul chose to remember what God had just brought him through.

The testimony of the storm was just a small part of the story. God proved Himself faithful to Paul yet again. What Paul had faith in was the word given to him by the Lord earlier.

The following night the Lord stood near Paul and said, "Take courage! As you have testified about me in Jerusalem, so you must also testify in Rome." (Acts 23:11, NIV)

Paul had the promise of God that he would make it to Rome. No amount of suffering, storm, shipwreck, or snakebite was going to hinder that. Paul's death was not part of God's plan.

Your life is the same. The fact that you have made it this far is a testimony! It's a testimony of your faithfulness, your hard work, your willingness to be stretched beyond your comfort zone, and your willingness to allow the Holy Spirit to work in and through you.

The sufferings of life will continue to come, and as they do, allow them to become symbols of what you will witness in your tomorrow.

Allow the work of God in your life. In the middle of clinging to a piece of wood in the storm, be built upon by God for an even greater future.

Allow the piece of wood to be a defining moment; don't toss it aside for what seems to be an easy way out. Allow God to use the storms of suffering to help you grow.

BIG IDEAS:

Times of suffering seem like huge hindrances and obstacles in our lives. However, God has a purpose and plan for these sufferings, and He will use them to help us grow.

GROUP STUDY QUESTIONS:

1. What is a trial or struggle that you are suffering through in your life?

2. The author said, "Too many Christians seek worldly advice for spiritual decisions." Have you done this in your life? How?

3. How can the Holy Spirit help you in your time of suffering?

4. How can you help someone else who is suffering?

5. How can worshipping in your time of suffering help you overcome?

6. After reading this chapter, what is one thing you will put into practice or one thing you will change in your life?

7. How can we, as a group, help you do this?

-11-

BEING A WORSHIPPER

By: Walter Smith

Suppose that you begin framing your ultimate dream house. Instead of using nails or construction screws to put the studs, headers, rafters, and trusses together, you use good 'ole American duct tape. The fact is that the house may stay together for a while with such construction material, but the chances are extremely high that the structure will eventually collapse and fall down. All because we did not 'frame' the house properly. All because we used the wrong "stuff."

So what happens to the man of God who wants to frame his life as a godly man, yet starts out doing it wrong?

Improper spiritual construction is even more disastrous than constructing our homes in the wrong manner.

Area building codes, regulations, ceiling heights, interior soffits, the size of door openings, the width of hallways, construction of stairways…these are all elements that must be considered in building and framing a house, a barn, or any structure.

A speed square, (20 oz.) hammer, carpenter's level, chalk line, tape measure, nail bag, circular saw, ladders, scaffolding, air guns are essential tools needed to build. Learning how to use these tools is also part of the process of building.

Tools and plans for building are necessary for constructing something that will last. The framework of any structure is crucial. It is the framework that shapes and forms the entire structure.

The frame of a house could be likened to the skeleton of that house. If it is strong it provides the necessary support for all that follows....the sheetrock, trim boards, roofing material and more. But if the frame is weak, no amount of expensive finishes will hide the flaws. Those perfectly plastered walls will begin to crack every time a door slams, the granite countertops will gradually fall out of level, the custom cabinets will not close properly, and the oak flooring will bounce and squeak like a rusty spring.

Shortcuts in framing are the biggest mistake anyone could make. Indeed, it may take time before the sagging, the bouncing, and the movement begin to show up, but it will show up.

In desiring to frame our godly character as men, worship is a key component. A life truly framed in worship to the Lord will be a life that will withstand anything that we may face on the journey from earth to glory.

The apostle Paul described true worship perfectly in Romans 12:1-2:

> *I urge you therefore, brethren, by the mercies of God to present your bodies a living and holy sacrifice, acceptable to God which is your spiritual service of worship. And do not be conformed to this world but be transformed by the renewing of your mind that you may prove what the will of God is, that which is good and acceptable, or well pleasing and perfect. (NASB):*

Lives framed around the principle of worship will withstand the assault of the enemy's onslaught.

By itself, a single piece of framing in constructing a house or any building is rather weak. It's only strong when connected to the other framing pieces. For this reason, the term "framing member" is used. For example, four framed walls are still unstable until the roof trusses or second-story subfloor is tied in on top. That's why extra bracing is needed to support walls during the framing process.

Our lives are exactly that way. We need extra support during the spiritual framing of our lives. It's not enough to merely show up at church once or twice a week. We need support from friends, family, and other relationships during the week to shape our existence....to reach the character of the godly examples we desire to become.

When you begin a framing project, it's critical that the framing starts out as plumb, level and square. If the wall framing ends up crooked, the finished wall will be crooked. If the framing is poorly done, then critical structural issues will plague the building either in the immediate or long-range future.

Too many men take shortcuts in building their lives---framing their lives in way that avoids the appropriate steps. Just as sloppy craftsmanship, inferior building materials, and not using the proper tools will certainly cause a structure to have significant problems, total repentance and turning from our former lives is an absolute must in properly framing our spiritual lives.

We cannot construct a life that will be pleasing to Christ while using leftover building components from previous builds (inferior building materials). We cannot frame a life of worship without following what the Word of God says about *"seeking God first and His Kingdom."* (Matthew 6:33, NIV)

In framing a life of worship, we must precisely follow the blueprint that the Lord has laid out for us. We must hammer out time to:

> *Study to show thyself approved unto God, a workman that needs not to be ashamed, rightly dividing the word of truth.* (2 Timothy 2:15, KJV)

As men it is imperative that we cut the boards and rip the planks that will make up the sub-floor upon which the rest of the building will be built. Everything in our lives must fit together. The framework of our entire life needs to be precisely erected as a structure built for worship to our God.

For a number of years after college, while pastoring a small church, I worked building upper-middle-class homes for professional doctors and lawyers in a dedicated subdivision of Hickory, NC. The developer, a man named Bill, owned the massive housing development that was set right off of Interstate 40 in western North Carolina. When he heard that I did carpentry, he sought me out.

Bill asked for my assistance with a project, one for a well-known area medical doctor, needing to be finished prior to Thanksgiving and Christmas. Various setbacks had already occurred with framing the house.

When I accepted the job, I worked alongside several other experienced carpenters. However, their work ethic did not match what Bill desired. He needed every person on the job site to give their complete best for the project to be finished on time.

The truth of the matter was that the other carpenters would take very frequent breaks. When Bill would go into town for supplies or material they would always sit down. Other times they would take a fifteen or twenty minute extra break. It wasn't until they saw Bill's truck turn the corner on the road below the development, that they would begin hammering nails again!

Because these carpenters did not take a sense of pride in their craftsmanship, some of the work they did was enough to "just get by." Their work was not the quality that Bill desired. Once we were almost finished with the project, the week before Christmas, Bill fired everyone on the job except for one other carpenter and myself.

We finished the house so that it would be ready for the doctor and his family for Christmas. However, there were extenuating issues with some of the original framing of the house that cropped up months later.

Pocket doors began to not close properly.

Cabinet doors were sticking.

There were squeaky floors from not enough adhesive and nails being applied during the construction process.

These problems were difficult to address once the house was completed. Yet, we had to try and resolve the issues for the homeowner to be satisfied. All of this extra work was necessary because the men building the structure had failed to properly build according to the builder's standard and to the area's code.

In the same way, God has a code that every man needs to build upon. He desires that we worship Him in "spirit and truth." This is how we build our lives correctly and according to His code.

> *Jesus said, "Yet a time is coming and has now come, when the true worshipers will worship the Father in the Spirit and in truth, for they are the kind of worshipers the Father seeks."* (John 4:23, NIV)

Worship operates in the present tense. True worshippers are not satisfied with waiting to praise God around the throne in heaven. The fact that we may have worshipped in the past, or that glorious worship awaits us in the future, is unsatisfactory. Now is the time to enter true worship.

Just as framing a house is a craft that is learned, our ability to worship is developed and learned through application and experience. Worship is not learned by reading books, taking classes, or going to seminars. Like the art of prayer, worship is learned by doing. Our entire lives should be lives of worship.

True worship is not something that can occur for one hour, one day a week on Sunday. True worship is a constructed, brick by brick, lifestyle of devotion to the Lord. It is day by day, hour by hour, and minute by minute.

A true life, framed for worship to God, is a life in continual subjection towards the God of love.

Such a life is built and framed with confession of sin, prayer, exaltation, praise, reverence, devotion, adoration, obedience, thankfulness, honor, submission, sacrifice, admiration and more.

We are grateful for His presence in our lives.

We are blessed by His unchanging nature.

We are indebted for Him keeping His promises, for His unceasing love and grace, for saving us, for His faithfulness (even when we aren't always faithful to Him).

Worship is a lifestyle, but worship goes deeper than a lifestyle. Worship, like framing a house or a building has to be who you are in the innermost part of your being. The key is what is underneath. Once again, it is the framework that supports all that is visible.

You cannot make yourself a worshipper any more than you can make yourself president. You must be conformed into the image of Christ which is the image of the worshipper.

A worshipper is someone who has daily fellowship with God. The way to frame godly character is to be conformed to Christ. This involves consistent times of prayer and reading the Word of God, coupled with fasting.

Fasting sharpens that ability to discern the voice of God. Fasting is a very vital, if not pivotal, tool in the worshippers' tool box for the man of God. Fasting hammers out the image of what it is that we are building our lives toward.

A life framed for worship requires humility.

A life built for worship will build with a humble and contrite heart.

We must come to the Lord with a clean heart, with no unconfessed sin coming between us and the Lord.

The blueprints for a life of worship will show the absolute need for sacrifice. When we give something that costs nothing, it is of little value. True worship requires that we give of our time, talent, gifts, and treasures (finances).

Responding positively in "framing" worship in our lives, rather than bemoaning the trying circumstances will cause us to grow in godly character. In many churches, men have been taught to work, to volunteer and to witness, but men have not been taught to worship.

Being a worshipper means that you are willing to be cut, framed, and crafted by the master carpenter. This is not an easy task.

When we learn to worship the Lord each and every moment, it will totally change the way we live our lives.

We must worship the Lord in our workplaces by being light to a dark world.

We need to worship God while at school, driving in our car, doing chores around the house, shopping, at church and in every area of life.

We worship the Lord in our day-to-day lives by obeying what Jesus said.

SO, how are you "framing" your life today in worship, to be a substructure that God would honor?

How is your life coming together, nail by nail, screw by screw, board by board, to be the structural support system the Lord needs?

Are you using the proper tools to build godly character by being a total worshipper, 24/7?

Is there more you can do? Is there more you should do? By all means, frame a godly character by being a worshipper!

BIG IDEA:

In framing our godly character as men, worship is a key component. A life truly framed in worship to the Lord will be a life that will withstand anything that we may face on the journey from earth to glory.

GROUP STUDY QUESTIONS:

1. Look at your life outside of Sunday morning. How do you spend your time?

2. What consumes your thoughts and your energy?

3. What are you passionate about? What are you most focused on in life? Your answers to those questions are a great indicator of your love for God.

4. Would you rather pursue money, material things, and a career, or would you rather pursue God above all else?

5. How would you respond to the statement: "In many churches men have been taught to work, to volunteer and to witness, but men have not really been taught to worship"?

6. Is that statement true of your church or fellowship? How could this be changed if that is so?

7. After reading this chapter, what is one thing you will put into practice or one thing you will change in your life?

8. How can we, as a group, help you do this?

BEING A SERVANT

By: Jim Pence

"In the Discipline of service there is also great liberty. Service allows us to say 'no!' to the world's games of promotion and authority. It abolishes our need and desire for a 'pecking order'."[1]

The Apostle Paul demonstrated a clear understanding of the world's false view of a pecking order. In the salutation of his letter to the Romans he wrote:

> *Paul, a servant of Christ Jesus, called to be an apostle and set apart for the gospel of God.* (Romans 1:1, NIV)

While the Christian community would want to elevate the position of apostleship, Paul first referred to himself as "a servant."

Not many were called to be apostles, but all are called to be servants. The fact that he referred to himself as both in his opening sentence shows the importance of each role. Many would strive to become an apostle, but not many would aspire to become a servant.

Jesus, Who called Paul to become an apostle, is the ultimate example of servanthood and of servant-leadership. That example was never more obvious than in John 13:2-17 where the account of Him washing His disciples' feet is recorded.

Verses three through five read:

> *Jesus knew that the Father had put all things under his power, and that he had come from God and was returning to God; so he got up from the meal, took off his outer clothing, and wrapped a towel around his waist. After that, he poured water into a basin and began to wash his disciples' feet, drying them with the towel that was wrapped around him.* (John 13:3-5, NIV)

A SERVANT KNOWS WHERE HE COMES FROM

Jesus knew where He had come from: *"He had come from God."* A servant of Christ Jesus never forgets where he has come from.

I came from a "nominal" Christian home – if there is such a thing. I went to Sunday school and church every Sunday until my junior year in high school. I went to VBS, participated in all the children's ministries, went through catechism (well, I hid in the closet or any other hiding place I could find in the basement of the church). I knew about Christ, but I didn't know Him. I believed that God the Father created us, Jesus the Son died for us, and the Holy Spirit was sent to us. But I had no clue what that meant for me at that time or for the future. I had "a form of godliness" but no power to live what I believed.

The summer between my junior and senior year of high school I joined a racing team that raced a sprint car at our local dirt track. That was my "present life," and I thought it would also be my future life as well.

A driver from the other side of the country came and began racing at our track. Through a series of events, that driver became a very vocal Christ-follower. It was through his testimony that I began to see that there was more to Christianity than what I had experienced up to that point. After seeing a Billy Graham movie with a couple friends, my wife and I both accepted Christ as our Lord and Savior, becoming lifelong Christ-followers.

That's where I came from. A servant never forgets where they've come from.

Some come from terrible backgrounds of drugs and violence. Others, like me, came from a rather calm and stable background. But if you know where you've come from, you'll appreciate what it took to get you where you are today and you will appreciate where you are going in the future. Because Jesus knew He had come from the Father, He was free to serve with nothing to prove.

A SERVANT KNOWS WHO GIVES HIM POWER

Jesus also knew what He had: *Jesus knew that the Father had put all things under his power.* (John 13:3, NIV)

He had the power to do anything. He had the power to choose. He had the power to serve. He knew from where that power came.

When you know where you've come from and you know who gave you the power, you don't have to play the world's "pecking order" games.

Mother Teresa, the great missionary to Calcutta once said, *"I belong to Jesus. He must have the right to use me without consulting me."* That kind of true servanthood is foundational in building the life of a servant. As in constructing a building, we must have a good foundation.

Following the foundation is the laying of the floor, the raising of the walls, and the building of the roof. In time, many structures begin to crumble at this point. Many deficiencies and weaknesses begin to be exposed. Maybe it is inferior material or poor workmanship or taking shortcuts to save time and money. Total destruction and collapse may not come for a long time, but the deficiency and weakness is there to remind us that something just isn't right.

If salvation is the foundation, servanthood is an integral part of the framing. When we believe that we are the masters of our own kingdom instead of the servants in Christ's Kingdom, a weakness is exposed. When we think that everyone should serve us rather than us joyfully serving others, a deficiency in thought has crept in.

Recorded in Mark 10:42-45 are Jesus' words to His disciples:

> *Jesus called them together and said, "You know that those who are regarded as rulers of the Gentiles lord it over them, and their high officials exercise authority over them. Not so with you. Instead, whoever wants to become great among you must be your servant, and whoever wants to be first must be slave of all. For even the Son of Man did not come to be served, but to serve, and to give his life as a ransom for many."* (NIV)

Earthly kings and earthly rulers lord it over their subjects, but then earthly kingdoms and earthly rulers come and go. We, as Christ-followers, belong to a kingdom that has no end. We follow a Ruler who has come to stay, who promised that He would never leave us nor forsake us. We serve the Son of Man who did not come to be served, but to serve. How can we possibly do anything less?

I didn't know it at the time (I was but a child of maybe ten or eleven years of age), when God used my burly, tough, hard-working, cement-breaking Uncle Cuppy to teach me a lesson in servanthood. It was a lesson that I have never forgotten in over fifty years.

Uncle Cuppy (his real name was Elwood) had his own cement business. He laid practically all of the sidewalks, built most of the porches, and poured a lot of the retaining walls in our small town. These were the days before jack-hammers. These were the days when it took a big, strong man with a sledge hammer to break up the old cement in preparation to pour the new. After every job, Uncle Cuppy would end up with a pickup truck bed full of broken cement.

One hot summer afternoon he "hired" my younger cousin and me to throw the cement off the back of his truck. Jokingly, as I remember it, I said that I would be the supervisor while my younger cousin would empty the truck. I worked just as hard as he did in the heat of that day, but when it came time for our pay my cousin was paid more. I had worked just as hard, but because I had exalted myself at the beginning of the job, and because my uncle honored hard work, he paid me according to my attitude.

That silent rebuke hurt at the moment, but I knew in my heart that my show of superiority had suffered a much needed adjustment. Today, I thank God that He used my Uncle Cuppy and a truck load of cement to teach me a lesson in true servanthood: that it is as much about the attitude as it is about the action.

Our attitudes, like the foundation of a building, are mostly unseen. Our actions, on the other hand, are like the floors, walls, and roof. Our actions are what people see. However, any attempts to deal with our actions without consideration toward our attitudes can be like covering over a cracked wall instead of repairing a sinking foundation which had caused the wall to crack in the first place.

A SERVANT KNOWS WHERE HE'S GOING

Jesus knew where He had come from, He knew the source of His power, and thirdly He knew where He was going: He was "returning to God."

That is our blessed hope, that one day we all, as believers, will return to God the Father and hear:

> *"Well done, good and faithful servant! You have been faithful with a few things; I will put you in charge of many things. Come and share your master's happiness!"* (Matthew 25:21, NIV)

Notice He said, *"Good and faithful servant,"* not good and faithful pastor, or good and faithful CEO, or good and faithful business owner, teacher, doctor, or any other occupation. You may have occupied any one of those positions, and you may have done it with excellence, but in the end it is not what we occupied, rather it is what occupied us.

First and foremost, we are servants.

That fact should occupy our spirits, our thoughts and our attitudes. We are servants who know who we are, who know where our power comes from, and who are returning to our Master. We are servants who have had the extreme privilege of serving the King of Kings.

We opened this chapter with a quote from Richard Foster, so let us close with another:

"Right here we must see the difference between choosing to serve and choosing to be a servant. When we choose to serve, we are still in charge. We decide whom we will serve and when we will serve. And if we are in charge, we will worry a great deal about anyone stepping on us, that is, taking charge over us.

But when we choose to be a servant, we give up the right to be in charge. There is great freedom in this. If we voluntarily choose to be taken advantage of, then we cannot be manipulated. When we choose to be a servant, we surrender the right to decide when we will serve. We become available and vulnerable." [2]

Settle it now men: we never were, we are not now, and we will never be in charge. But when we know Who is, it is all okay because we know that we can trust Him with our very lives. We are, as Paul wrote, servants of Jesus Christ.

BIG IDEA:

God never called anyone to be a king; he called us ALL to be servants. A man of God should be known as a man who serves.

GROUP STUDY QUESTIONS:

1. What does it mean to be a servant?

2. The author said, "A servant of Christ Jesus never forgets where he has come from." What does this mean to you?

3. What role does gratitude play in being a servant?

4. How can the Holy Spirit help you in your time of suffering?

5. What hinders you from being a servant?

6. After reading this chapter, what is one thing you will put into practice or one thing you will change in your life?

7. How can we, as a group, help you do this?

13

BUILDING GODLY CHARACTER— DISCIPLESHIP

By: David Twiss

A professional framer possesses good disciplines in their work. They have a set way of doing things. There are little "tricks of the trade" that they have discovered in their time as a framer. However, it is not just skills or abilities that make a good framer.

When a person wants a house built, they generally would like a timetable for the project. The framer will have to set a schedule on when they will be there, what the length of their day will be, and how much work it will take to get the job done in a timely manner. Questions that would need to be answered would be things such as:

What time will we start working, and how many hours will we work daily?

How many workers will be necessary to accomplish the job?

What materials will we need?

Will I need to rent any tools?

These questions that our framer wrestles with are similar to the question in a believer's life about discipleship. In the same way that a builder constructs a frame that will serve as the skeleton of all that the house will become, the believer constructs their spiritual lives within the frame of discipleship. Discipleship would be the way that you accomplish the work of building that spiritual house.

Similarly to the question that a framer has to answer, a disciple should ask themselves the same type of questions:

Do you show up on time each day and work through the day?

Is your work different from day-to-day, or do you have a set type of work that you do each day?

Do you stay up-to-date on the latest tools and innovations to help you create this masterpiece?

Are you including others in this project, and are you sharing your experiences and the wisdom that you have gained with them?

Webster's dictionary defines a disciple as, "Someone who accepts and helps to spread the teachings of a famous person."[1] Discipleship would be the process that somebody uses to accomplish serving as a disciple.

Today, there are a lot of resources and thoughts about discipleship. You cannot peruse through Christian magazines, television, radio, or websites without hearing much about the importance of discipleship. The word discipleship brings various things to many different people's minds.

Many pastors cringe when asked, "What is your church's discipleship method?" Other people feel guilty because they do not have a set discipleship program in which they are involved. Let's look at a few models of discipleship.

MODELS OF DISCIPLESHIP

1. JESUS MODEL

Jesus used the phrase, "Follow me" in securing disciples.

The call was then either answered or rejected by the person being called.

For the twelve disciples, this process was a 24/7 commitment that continued over a period of about three years. They spent great amounts of time traveling, eating, and living life with the Savior. For the 70 disciples, this process would not take quite as long or be as in-depth. There were also other followers of Christ who weren't part of the disciples, yet they followed Him.

2. THE EARLY CHURCH MODEL

They devoted themselves to the apostles' teaching and to fellowship, to the breaking of bread and to prayer. Everyone was filled with awe at the many wonders and signs performed by the apostles. All the believers were together and had everything in common. They sold property and possessions to give to anyone who had need. Every day they continued to meet together in the temple courts. They broke bread in their homes and ate together with glad and sincere hearts, praising God and enjoying the favor of all the people. And the Lord added to their number daily those who were being saved. (Acts 2:42-47, NIV)

This model shows the effectiveness of the early church. Here, discipleship was accomplished by living life daily together with the apostles and other believers, eating together, praying together, serving together, giving together, and learning together. Once again the model called for daily expressions and occurrences.

3. EARLY TWENTIETH CENTURY DISCIPLESHIP

In the early days of Twentieth Century Pentecost, discipleship looked a little like the early church model. Church pretty much consisted of meeting all day on Sunday, with many churches eating a meal and spending the day together. Special services, revivals, and prolonged seasons of fasting and prayer were the norm. Daily study of the Bible and disciplines of prayer were seen as key ways to accomplish being a disciple. A rejection of worldly entertainment and a dedication to godly things were promoted. Accessing the power of the Holy Spirit was seen as fundamental in living this victorious life.

4. MID-TWENTIETH CENTURY DISCIPLESHIP

By the middle of the 20th century, there were many helps for believers in discipleship. Bible studies became very common and were available in great number at little cost. Resources such as Berean School of the Bible and other correspondence Bible studies became available. The technology of radio and television brought teaching into homes. There was also the development of many translations of the Scriptures, as well as chronological and daily Bible reading sources and a plethora of Christian books.

As the century progressed, the Internet made many other resources available to the believer. I remember back in the 1980s when Larry Lea launched the movement that was based off of Christ's question to His disciples in the garden: "Could you not tarry one hour?" This movement promoted waking up early and spending an hour in prayer before your day began.

In all of these models of discipleship, there is a vein of truth running throughout. Yet, the reality is that discipleship is accomplished when we discipline ourselves daily to do what we know to do. The important thing is to have a plan, and stick to that plan.

Going back to the example of the builder, the builder generally has a set start time, and quite possibly a finish time for each day on the job. There are set tasks that they will set out to do, and will not be satisfied until those tasks are accomplished. In the same way, discipleship needs to be that type of priority in a believer's life.

A well-rounded discipleship plan would incorporate developing spiritual disciplines such as: reading the Bible, prayer, serving, giving, fellowship with others of like faith, thanksgiving to the Father, fellowship with Christ, and communing with the Holy Spirit.

PITFALL OF MAKING DISCIPLESHIP SIMPLY INTELLECTUAL

I do believe that there is a mistake that we make in modern times in thinking that discipleship is simply studying and acquiring knowledge.

I know that we are told in 2 Timothy 2:15 to:

Be diligent (study) to present yourself approved to God, a worker who does not need to be ashamed, rightly dividing the word of truth. (NKJV)

For many, this has become the sum total of discipleship. However, discipleship goes beyond just learning and intellectually understanding Scriptures.

Back in the 1980s, when the "Tarry for One Hour" movement arose, I found myself going through rigors of discipleship for the wrong reasons. I was doing them because I felt obligated and guilty if I wasn't doing what others felt I should do. The idea of me contributing in a relationship with my Savior was secondary to personal pride and accomplishment.

Serving Christ should not be a "ball and chain" that we are obligated to wear. It is walking in love and growing in grace, knowledge, and relationship with the One Who loves us with an everlasting love.

The object of discipleship should never be completion of a resource, such as a devotional, but rather working toward maturity and the completion of our own character and godliness. Jesus tells us to:

Be perfect, therefore, as your heavenly Father is perfect. (Matt. 5:48, NIV)

The word "perfect" in that passage means, according to Strong's Concordance, "Complete (in various applications of labor, growth, mental and moral character, etc.); - of full age."[2] This occurs and is accomplished through the process of well-rounded discipleship.

When we relegate discipleship to simply being an intellectual exercise, we miss the mark. Our salvation is not simply knowledge about the Savior, but is truly a living, vibrant relationship with our Savior. We have access to the Father through this sacrifice of the Son empowered by the Holy Spirit.

When we look at those biblical models of discipleship, we see that although learning was part of the process, it was only part of the process. True biblical discipleship would incorporate learning, but wouldn't end with it.

Paul counsels us to, "*Pray without ceasing*" (1 Thess. 5:17, KJV).

It would also incorporate prayer, but wouldn't end with that either. It contains anointed teaching, fellowship, eating, charity and giving, worshipping together, godly friendships, and praising the Lord. When you look at your life and take stock in your discipleship process, see how many facets of biblical discipleship you are incorporating.

Discipleship is the process by which we accomplish growth, character, and productivity in the Kingdom of God.

In some ways, discipleship is not something that we do as much as it is a characteristic of a lifestyle of who we are as followers of Jesus Christ!

Be diligent in loving and serving the Master Builder as well as your fellow builders in the Kingdom!

BIG THOUGHT:

Discipleship is not just something we do; it is a lifestyle of all who call themselves followers of Jesus Christ.

GROUP STUDY QUESTIONS:

1. What is the first thing that comes to mind when thinking about discipleship?

2. Do you have a regular personal discipleship process?

3. How does your process compare to the biblical method of the early church?

4. Have you relegated discipleship to a simple process of information gathering and made the process of discipleship into a simply intellectual process?

5. What can you do to better diversify discipleship in your life to a greater balanced approach?

6. After reading this chapter, what is one thing you will put into practice or one thing you will change in your life?

7. How can we, as a group, help you do this?

14

BUILDING ACCOUNTABILITY

By: Jamie Holden

Many people don't know this about me, but I'm a pretty good handyman. For about five years of my life, God took me through a time where my life pretty much revolved around remodeling our family's home.

We gutted everything! We added new windows, new doors, new flooring… everything you can imagine we did to the house. We even added on a one room addition.

While we were doing these projects, I quickly learned that two pairs of eyes were better than one when it came to things like cutting, measuring trim, or cutting the length of a board. I have to admit, when I first got started, I hated it when my dad would ask me to measure things twice or if he asked me, "Are you sure that's the right measurement for that piece of wood that we need?"

My rebellious side kind of reared up inside of me, and I would think, "Listen Dad, I know what I'm doing! I don't need you to hold me accountable for every single piece of wood I cut!"

However, as I quickly learned, having somebody else helping you measure and having another pair of eyes showing you the way to do things really was a good benefit. I didn't know everything I thought I knew. I wasn't as perfect as I thought I was. When you're cutting expensive lumber and expensive trim, you don't want to make a lot of mistakes. You need somebody coming alongside of you, showing you how to do it, holding you accountable, and just showing you the ropes.

Just like in homebuilding, in the Christian walk you need to have accountability.

I believe every man of God needs to have at least one man who holds him accountable---a man that will hold his feet to the fire. A man who is able and willing to ask the hard questions that you don't really want to hear and don't want to answer.

Why is this so important?

Well, the truth is that none of us is perfect. We all have things that we need to change in our lives. We all have character flaws and issues that we can't recognize inside of ourselves. We need another mentor, another man, coming alongside of us and helping us discover our weak spots.

We need to have men in our lives who are aware of the problems we have, the struggles, temptations, and bondages that hold us captive. We need to allow these men to ask us any questions at any time in our life. They need to have free reign with us to go where we don't want anybody else going.

Sounds uncomfortable right?

Yeah, it is uncomfortable. But that's the point!

You want somebody being that tough on you. You want somebody holding you accountable. You need it so you can keep growing in your spiritual walk with God.

I'm a firm believer that every man needs to have a man in his life that he meets with periodically who is allowed to ask him some of the really hard questions. Personally, I meet with my mentor once a month and we talk on the phone or text in between.

So in what areas should a man be held accountable with a mentor?

YOUR WALK WITH GOD

We need to have a mentor who holds our feet to the flame and asks tough questions like:

Are you spending time in the Word of God?

Are you spending time in prayer?

How's your church attendance been?

Are you gathering together with your band of brothers and men's ministry?

We need a man holding us accountable and helping us through the day-to-day routine of prayer and Bible reading. Most of us aren't going to do it on our own, we need another man holding us accountable.

Last year, one of the speakers at a Mantour Men's Conference told a story about how, when he was in college, he had another man start holding him accountable. This man would always ask him, "Have you read the Bible today?," "Did you pray?," "Are you spending time in the Word?".

The young college guy wasn't really that concerned about these areas, he had a lot of stuff to do. Still, he started reading the Bible because he got tired of having to say "no."

He knew the guy was going to ask and he would have to give an answer. As a result, studying the Bible became a part of his daily routine. How many know when a man gets something into his routine, it becomes a part of him?

This speaker developed this pattern of Bible study in his life because his mentor held him accountable. Accountability is SO important!

131

YOUR THOUGHT LIFE

We all need to have another man holding us accountable when it comes to staying pure. That's why I'm such a believer in programs like Covenant Eyes---programs that block Internet porn from your phone, computer, or any device you're using.

What's really great about Covenant Eyes is that that it allows an accountability feature where your mentor is sent an email showing them what you're doing online. This accountability is so important to help men stay pure. I encourage all men to check out Covenant Eyes. To help you get started, you can find a promo code to save money on the Mantour Ministries website.

Yet even beyond technology, men need other men holding them accountable in their thought life. You need men in your life saying to you:

What are you watching?

What are you looking at on your computer?

What movies and TV are you watching that you know you shouldn't be watching?

Are you having thoughts about people and women in your life that you should not be having?

These are uncomfortable questions, but we need to have this accountability in our life.

OUR RELATIONSHIPS

Each of us needs another man who will hold us accountable when it comes to relationships. If you're married, you need somebody to hold you accountable asking questions like:

Are you spending the time with your wife?

Are you having good communication with your wife?

If you have kids:

Are you being a good father?

How much time have you given to your kids?

We need to be held accountable to help us see if our work or our activities are causing us to spend more time with those things than we are with our family.

If you're single, you need guys holding you accountable with your relationships. You need someone asking you:

Are you treating your girlfriend with respect?

Are you pressuring her in any way to do things that she shouldn't be doing?

Are you doing anything to encourage her to grow in her walk with God?

We need to have this accountability in our relationships.

FINANCIALLY

Nobody likes to have somebody else's nose in their money, right? However, it is important we have accountability when it comes to our finances.

I am a huge believer that all men need to have somebody else involved in their finances.

If you're married, your wife must be an equal partner with you in the finances. She needs to know what's going on with your finances, how much money you have, what your budget is, and how your money is being spent.

No man can do this job alone...he needs accountability. If you're single, you need to find somebody, a trusted friend or mentor, to help you be accountable financially.

Money is too big of a trap, and too many men find themselves trapped in secrets and lies. That's why accountability is a must when it comes to our finances

As we bring this chapter to a close, I want to list a few questions for you to use when you meet with your mentor. These are 10 questions every mentor should ask you, and, if you're mentoring another man, you need to ask them these 10 questions.

1. Have you had your devotions faithfully?

2. What did God teach you through His Word this last week?

3. Have you exposed your mind to sexually inappropriate things? Did you look at any porn or watch anything you shouldn't have watched?

4. What sin did you battle with this week?

5. Did God give you victory in an unexpected way?

6. What do you anticipate will be a battle in the coming week?

7. Are you being honest with others?

8. How is your family life?

9. Are you exercising and taking care of your body?

10. Have you lied to me about any of your answers?

These questions, coupled with the questions listed with each point we discussed, are excellent ways to help you be accountable.

Just like when you're building a house and you need a foreman or a fellow worker helping you be accountable and making sure you're doing the work correctly, you need a man in your life to hold you accountable in all areas of your walk with God, your relationships, your family, your finances, and your thought life.

As you're growing in your walk with God, you need to remember your life is under construction and you need to have other people helping you along the way.

So I strongly encourage every man reading this to find a mentor and let them hold you accountable. Make accountability a huge cornerstone of your walk with God!

BIG IDEA:

You need a man in your life to hold you accountable in all areas of your walk with God, your relationships, your family, your finances, and your thought life.

GROUP STUDY QUESTIONS:

1. Why is accountability important?

2. What is your biggest fear about having an accountability partner?

3. Do you have someone holding you accountable? If not, who is someone you could ask to hold you accountable?

4. Why is it important to be held accountable in our daily spiritual disciplines?

5. Why is it important to have someone else holding you financially accountable?

6. After reading this chapter, what is one thing you will put into practice or one thing you will change in your life?

7. How can we, as a group, help you do this?

-15-

FINDING PURPOSE IN YOUR WORK

By: Jamie Zirkle

In Rick Warren's book, "The Purpose Driven Life", he begins by saying that "it's not about you."[1]

Men, the purpose in your work is not about you, and it's not about me. We were not created for ourselves, but for the Lord.

The purpose in our work is to bring glory and honor to the Lord. It's the central question that should be ringing through our ears every day at work, "Am I bringing honor to the Lord right now?"

Yes, I believe God wants us to work hard. I believe He wants us to make money. I believe He wants us to be happy at our jobs. I believe that He wants us to provide for our families. But, none of that matters to God if we aren't working hard to glorify Him.

There is a passage of Scripture that sums up all of this perfectly:

> *Whatever you do, work at it with all your heart, as working for the Lord, not for human masters, since you know that you will receive an inheritance from the Lord as a reward. It is the Lord*

Christ you are serving. (Colossians 3:23-24, NIV)

At the start of your next shift, this verse needs to be at the forefront of your mind.

A few years ago, I was in between jobs. In fact, since 2007 my wife and I have been through a combined four job layoffs. Some of you can relate. But, it was in the summer of 2013 that I made the decision to leave my role as a youth pastor and pursue another ministry avenue that did not end up working out.

At the end of that summer, I was without a job. A friend of mine who owned a local Subway franchise offered me a job. I knew that this job would not pay anywhere close to what I was making as a youth pastor, but I needed a job.

Have you ever had a job that you didn't want to work? This was me at Subway.

Early on, I have to admit that I wasn't too thrilled about getting up at 5am to open the store. I really struggled with finding the purpose in baking bread or asking someone if they wanted their sub toasted or not.

My perspective changed one day when an older lady came into the store to get her husband his lunch for the day. He was a mail carrier. She had this grin on her face at 7 a.m. that annoyed me. Who in the world is grinning ear to ear at 7 a.m.?

We struck up a conversation, and we found out that she was one of my elementary school teachers! I began to open up to her and tell her my story. She listened politely for a few minutes as I rambled on and on about the past few months, and then she suddenly stopped me and asked, "Whose team do you play for?"

With a puzzled look on my face, she deducted that I did not understand the question. She asked me the same question this way, "Who is your coach? Do you play for God or for man?"

I said, "God."

She smiled, paid for her sub, and then she left.

It was in that moment that I realized how selfish I was. God had opened a door for me to work at this job. He knew this was not what I went to school for, and He knew that it would only be for a season, but I made it all about me.

From that day forward I worked hard to change my attitude and to recognize that my purpose was to bring honor to the Lord. There are countless stories that I can tell about the many people that came into that store over the fourteen months that I worked there. Those divine appointments will always stay with me.

Luke says: *"If you are faithful in little things, you will be faithful in large ones. But if you are dishonest in little things, you won't be honest with greater responsibilities."* (Luke 16:10, NLT)

So, how do you find the purpose in your work? What's the magic formula? What's the secret sauce to this recipe? It is one word: faithfulness.

When I think of faithfulness, I think of one person and that is Joseph. His story can be found in the book of Genesis in chapters 37-50.

Joseph was the eleventh son of Jacob. He was known to be a tattletale, an arrogant seventeen-year-old, and just so happened to be a daddy's boy. His father favored him more than his other sons. In fact, this is the same Joseph who would receive a colorful new coat from his father.

His brothers resented him so much that they plotted to kill him. However, Reuben, the oldest son comes up with another plan; they would sell him into slavery. He was sold to a high ranking Egyptian by the name of Potiphar.

The Bible says that Joseph was favored by God and so Potiphar put him in charge of his entire household. One day Potiphar's wife comes on to him, and Joseph flees, but he is falsely accused of rape and thrown into prison.

Potiphar was furious when he heard his wife's story about how Joseph had treated her. So he took Joseph and threw him into the prison where the king's prisoners were held, and there he remained.

But the Lord was with Joseph in the prison and showed him his faithful love. And the Lord made Joseph a favorite with the prison warden. Before long, the warden put Joseph in charge of all the other prisoners and over everything that happened in the prison. The warden had no more worries, because Joseph took care of everything. The Lord was with him and caused everything he did to succeed. (Genesis 39:19-23, NLT)

Joseph was faithful in Potiphar's house, and he brought glory and honor to the Lord when he refused the advances of his boss' wife. It may seem unfair that Joseph was sent to prison, but God had a plan. Many years would pass and Joseph continued to remain faithful in the small things. I'm sure he had his sleepless nights. I bet he felt homesick. I can guarantee you that he was anxious to get out of that cell.

And one day he did.

Pharaoh needed a dream interpreted, and a former prisoner happened to remember Joseph interpreting one of his a few years ago. When Pharaoh saw that God was with Joseph, he decided to make him second in command of all of Egypt.

Years later, when a famine would hit the land and Joseph's family came looking for food, guess who was there to feed his family? Joseph.

You may be a pastor of a church. You may be a CEO of a large organization. You may be a janitor. You may be a school teacher. You may work at Subway or you may be in prison.

I want you to know that God is with you and His desire is for you. His purpose for you in the work that you do is to bring glory and honor to Him. You do that by being faithful. In whatever task God has assigned you, do as the author of Colossians says to do and "work as unto the Lord."

That is the purpose in your work.

BIG IDEA:

The main reason we work is to bring glory and honor to God. We need to be honest in our work, always remembering that our actions reflect God to our unsaved co-workers. We are called to bring God honor and be faithful in our day-to-day job.

GROUP STUDY QUESTIONS:

1. What lessons can you learn from the story of Joseph that would help you in finding purpose in your work? Are there any other Biblical examples that come to mind?

2. What do you believe the purpose in your own work is?

3. What purpose do you believe God has for you at your current job?

4. Is there someone at your church or your job site that you can talk to confidentially about this?

5. What steps can you make, today, to begin to find the purpose in your work? What challenges will you face when making those steps? How will you work through those challenges?

6. How can we, as a group, help you do this?

16

SUCCESS THAT MATTERS

By: Joey Cullen

We live in a world that is filled with a myriad of potential disappointments, in which people are consumed with pleasing those that are of no concern.

"People pleasing" propels us to wonder if we said the right words or took the right action to ensure that we do not experience disappointment from those whom we wish to receive affirmation.

People of all nations, religions, and walks of life hide behind a face painted with confidence, concealing the fear of being seen as one who may not have their life all together. Living behind this illusion breeds insecurity, as we are gripped with the fear of disappointing those we have deemed "worthy" of granting acceptance and approval.

Insecurity and fear are often lurking behind an independent front; we appear to not care about other people's opinion of us, even motivating us to degrade those whom we believe to be expendable.

High school students may see the chance to top another student just to gain the respect of someone who "matters" more.

To gain a promotion at work, an individual may become more diligent in his or her work productivity than another co-worker seeking the same promotion.

These types of small and hollow successes in life will ultimately determine our future success.

Galatians 6:7 clearly states: *Do not be deceived: God cannot be mocked. A man reaps what he sows.* (NIV)

When we choose to sow deceptions, mockery, and such, we will, in return, reap the same.

As the fear of disappointing others affects your relationships, ultimately your relationship with God is adversely impacted. Whatever extreme a person is willing to go to maintain what he sees as natural success, will transfer over to how he finds his success in God, if not careful.

Gossipers and back biters still cause damage in the church today, attempting to bring about their own success at the expense of God's glory. They try to tear down others for their own shallow reward.

When a person is saved, God washes away every sin, just as 1 Corinthians 6:11 says. However, old, ingrained habits now need to be changed by God's power. Sanctification is a process by which a person must continually depend on grace, relying on the Holy Spirit every day to build them up and become the person of God He desires us to be.

Building construction is analogous to the sanctification process in the believer. One must be sure that in the construction of a building and a life for God's glory, the foundation is sturdy enough to withstand the pressure and weight of the building.

A building and the Christian life must be built with quality materials to prevent a devastating collapse. Use of substandard materials weakens both an edifice and the Christian. Carefully, beams need to be set in the correct places, bolts need to be tightened, and the quality of material will ultimately make or break the building.

When you use cheap material you may look good for a while, but eventually your building will falter. One must be sure that in the construction of the building, the foundation is sturdy enough to withhold the pressure and weight of the building.

Matthew 7:24-27 says:

> *Therefore everyone who hears these words of mine and puts them into practice is like a wise man who built his house on the rock. The rain came down, the streams rose, and the winds blew and beat against that house; yet it did not fall, because it had its foundation on the rock. But everyone who hears these words of mine and does not put them into practice is like a foolish man who built his house on sand. The rain came down, the streams rose, and the winds blew and beat against that house, and it fell with a great crash.* (NIV)

The success you value will ultimately decide your future state of being.

Some may think that because they were saved their view of success automatically changes, but this is not true.

Should it change?

Of course it should.

What matters as a whole should be completely altered as a person grows in God.

For as we grow to become like Jesus, we start to think more like Jesus, see more like Jesus, and hopefully act more like Jesus. If the way we thought before we got saved was the perfect way of thinking then salvation was not needed; and if how we think now is the perfect way of thinking, then grace and guidance is not necessary.

The issue is: how MUCH of us will be saved, i.e. become more like Jesus?

Coming to an altar or raising our hand to ask Jesus into our life is only the very beginning. Transformation is a lifetime process that saves us from the destructive effects of our poor choices, while promising us eternity in God's presence.

Through periods of my life I felt insecure in my ability to teach, preach, and even do things like write the chapter for this book. My insecurity stemmed from the questions of what qualified me for such roles. I am encouraged and motivated when I see the reality of who has called me, alongside the assurance of Isaiah 55:11:

> *So is my word that goes out from my mouth: It will not return to me empty, but will accomplish what I desire and achieve the purpose for which I sent it.* (NIV)

In my life, I have thought of many ideas that did not work out, spoke to people in ways I maybe should not have, and lived my life in ways that may not have been pleasing to the Lord. However, one thing I have always based my life on is the fact that my life is not perfect, but God is not looking for perfect people. He is looking for willing people who understand they have not yet arrived; teachable people, always looking to change and grow, as well as being willing to be used in any capacity.

2 Timothy 2:21 says, *Those who cleanse themselves from the latter will be instruments for special purposes, made holy, useful to the Master and prepared to do any good work.* (NIV)

I am a mortal vessel, a marred piece of pottery. As an imperfect piece of pottery, the potter is always putting me on the potter's wheel to make me new.

As Isaiah 64:8 says: *Yet you, LORD, are our Father. We are the clay, you are the potter; we are all the work of your hand.* (NIV)

And at times, because we are being stretched, molded, and shaped, it may seem as if we are doing most of the work. Yet, remember God is the real One working, all we have to do is make space and let Him work.

1 Corinthian 6:19 says: *Do you not know that your bodies are temples of the Holy Spirit, who is in you, whom you have received from God? You are not your own.* (NIV)

In order to be an effective instrument used by God, we must do to our temple what Jesus did to the temple in John 2: drive out all that does not belong there.

When a man thinks he is the one who brings success, then a humbling experience is on its way.

Throughout the Bible, we see recurrences of people thinking they can take the glory from God: Satan being cast out of Heaven for desiring to be like God, Saul taking the place of God's prophet, Samuel thinking he could force God's voice, and even Ananias and Sapphira thinking they could lie to the Holy Spirit. In all reality, when we act on our own behalf because we think we know best, we play God; and that's a dangerous place to be.

Now, there is a level of success that could come with that. Business men of the world make decisions on their own behalf to become successful. All over the world, even preachers, teachers, those who consider themselves people of God, make a conscious choice to do what they need to do to get rich, gaining what they think is prosperity, and amassing material wealth. But, is their acquisition of worldly gain considered real success in God's eyes?

A false notion in Christianity makes its rounds in believers' thinking: "If I am truly blessed by God, I will be wealthy, and never have a financial struggle." The idea is false, for if material gain were the benchmark, it would mean that success can only be measured by how full your pockets are. Worldly success and spiritual success are measured in two completely different ways.

Worldly success can be measured by wealth and materials. Spiritual success is measured by whether or not we are doing the will of God.

Does this mean it's God will for people to be poor?

According to Scripture, I believe God does not require one to be poor or rich, in regard to worldly wealth. He only requires for us to be poor in spirit as Matthew 5:3 states.

Being poor in spirit means that we cannot do anything without God. This makes a person wholly dependent on God.

1 Corinthians 3:7 says: *So neither the one who plants nor the one who waters is anything, but only God, who makes things grow.* (NIV)

We are ambassadors, here only to do the will of Him who created us. Any other successes aside from doing His will are not successes that matter for eternity.

We can have all the success this world has to offer, but when we see Jesus face to face, it's the success that matters to Him that He will be looking for and hopefully find in us.

If a person seeks to be truly successful as a Christian, he must first understand these 4 things:

---Serving God means that you may disappoint other at times.

---You are always under construction.

---Make sure your foundation is sturdy.

---You are only an instrument, a vessel used by God. God is the One Who brings the success!

BIG IDEA:

True success isn't having fame, wealth, or things. True success is defined as whether or not we are doing God's will for our lives.

GROUP STUDY QUESTIONS:

1. What are you doing to assure success in your life?

2. Evaluate your life. Write down a list of your top 5 priorities starting with your most important. Where does God fit in that list?

3. What material are you using to assure your building/life will stand strong?

4. What steps are you taking to ensure your foundation is solid?

5. As the temple of the Holy Spirit, how are you cooperating with Him to get rid of what is hindering you, to better allow the Spirit to have His way?

6. After reading this chapter, what is one thing you will put into practice or one thing you will change in your life?

7. How can we, as a group, help you do this?

17

LIVING A HEALTHY LIFE

By: Anthony Pelella

Recently, I had a friend tell me about an experience he had while doing evangelist work at a conference. My friend, who keeps himself in good shape, was taken back when a "point of view" was shared with him from another person attending. He approached my friend with this observation: "Why should I listen to the preacher when he tells me to watch what comes out of my mouth," he said about the guest speaker, "when it's obvious he does not watch what he puts into his?"

The man pointed out how undisciplined the eating habits of this pastor were because of his appearance, and it caused him to feel the preacher was hypocritical in his words since both the body and soul are important to God. He felt the preacher's lack of self-control physically made him have no right to tell him he needed self control spiritually. My friend lovingly tried to put things into perspective for this man and "had the guest speaker's back."

Although this topic of eating healthy and exercising may not seem spiritual to many who read this, please know that nothing could be further from the truth.

We often teach about what we allow into our heart via our eyes. How detrimental it is for us to expose ourselves to ungodly and perverse things that this world feels comfortable embracing.

We would quote Psalm 101:3, "*I will not look with approval on anything that is vile*," (NIV) as a reference to follow the Word and not our fleshly tendencies. Yet, why do we dismiss the lack of integrity we show by the way we take care of the one body we will ever have while on this earth? We reject so much sin that we once celebrated such as pornography, cursing, rage, etc... yet, we have justified or ignored the fact that we embrace the "one thing" everyone is comfortable with... gluttony.

This is indeed dangerous and has adverse effects on us as people, who, as children of the King, should be enjoying life and health in every aspect of the terms. How many times have we had to pray for someone who had issues with their heart, lungs, blood pressure etc...because they refused to show self control over what they put in their mouth? Think of all the unnecessary disease we see in the church because it seems that no one cares about the sugar, salt, GMO's (Genetically Modified Organisms) and so on that is loaded in all the food most people love.

Don't get me wrong, I understand that you can eat and train like an Olympian and still get sick or injured. That's understood, but so much of the sickness that we deal with in our world today is self-inflicted and could be avoided through healthy living.

So, if we are going to be vigilant about the soul, it makes sense that we would take care of the body since it is God's command to us. Remember, Jesus told his disciples to teach the future disciples to OBEY EVERYTHING that He had taught them.

So what do the Scriptures tell us about how our bodies should be treated?

> *Do you not know that your bodies are temples of the Holy Spirit, who is in you, whom you have received from God? You are not*

your own; you were bought at a price. Therefore honor God with your bodies. (1 Corinthians 6:19-20, NIV)

Of course this passage means that we are to live a Christ-like life, but does it end there? Is it possible to honor God with our bodies by keeping it healthy?

Although smoking is not mentioned in the Bible, we have a huge problem with it because we know that it is slowly killing the person who chooses to do so. Why do we think it's wrong? Because they are killing the one body God gave us to be good stewards over.

The Bible also has a word for eating however and whenever we please. It's called gluttony!! Think about the similarities:

---We pollute our bodies with unhealthy food while a smoker pollutes with cigarettes.

---We slowly experience a change physiologically... i.e. weight gain. (You can smell a person who smokes, see their yellow teeth and fingernails etc...)

---Over time, not only do we see evidence of our poor eating on the outside, but inside all types of sickness is developing. (For a smoker this may be lung cancer, gluttony may be diabetes, heart disease etc...)

So why do we take such a strong stance against smoking but "turn the cheek" when it comes to gluttony? I guess that's a similar question the young man in the beginning of this chapter would like to know.

Next, pay attention to this truth:

> *Their destiny is destruction, their god is their stomach, and their glory is in their shame...their mind is set on earthly things.* (Philippians 3:19, NIV)

Paul was talking about the heathen nations around Israel at the time. Look at what was seen to be their god, their stomach!

Wow, their eating habits and desire for pleasure through food showed what was most important to them. Remember, Israel was given dietary laws for a reason. It kept them healthy and separate from the habits and certain lifestyles of the nations around them.

Yes, Paul told us in Philippians 4:13 that we can do all things in Christ, but in the chapter before he did not say that we can eat all things!!!

How or what should we eat according to the Scriptures?

> *Then God said, "I give you every seed-bearing plant on the face of the whole earth and every tree that has fruit with seed in it. They will be yours for food."* (Genesis 1:29, NIV)

The menu gets expanded in Genesis 9:3:

> *Everything that lives and moves about will be food for you. Just as I gave you the green plants, I now give you everything.* (NIV)

The key word here for us is LIVING!! The foods we consume should not have a shelf life of thirty years or turn into fiberglass when we heat up the "cream filling." We should be putting nutrients into our bodies that bring life, and we should be doing it in moderation. Have a good meal filled with calories once in awhile, but it should be the rule not the norm!!

This chapter was just a foundational challenge to help you realize the importance of living a healthy life. Too many people, Christian and non-Christian alike, have forfeited living a strong vibrant life which God intended for them because of poor eating habits and lack of activity.

When speaking of David, the Bible says in 1 Chronicles 29:28:

> *He died at a good old age, having enjoyed long life, wealth and honor. His son Solomon succeeded him as king.* (NIV)

I don't know about you, but if the Lord does not return in our lifetime, I don't want to live my life being filled with disease or unable to enjoy playing games with friends or kids because of my undisciplined lifestyle choices. I want to die at a good old age, having enjoyed long life!!

> *For physical training is of some value...* (1 Timothy 4:8, NIV)

154

Although this passage goes on to tell us godliness is much better, the physical aspects do have value! This points out that it's not just about eating right, but actually training or taking care of our body by being active!!

Isaiah 40:31 tells us to soar, run, walk…in other words God wants us to always be moving forward. We need to do the same physically, as well as spiritually. Being active is very important to stay strong and healthy.

Recently, I saw a picture of two women in their mid-seventies. One lady was posing for a fitness competition and was in amazing shape. The other lady was in a chair, hunched over and in need of a walker.

What happened? How could there be such a difference?

One woman stayed active and kept moving forward, the other became sedentary and let her body slowly start to break down due to lack of motion.

It is amazing to me how similar the body and the spirit of man are; how they respond to the same type of stimuli to get us to grow. I personally like to show those that I preach to, not only the spiritual truths of God's Word, but also personal application.

In my life, I have had two passions that bring this to light: Jesus and bodybuilding. I am amazed that the very things we do to make our bodies grow, Christ also does in us to get us to grow spiritually. This is what being healthy is all about. If we, as believers, have a bad "walk" with God we will be seen as someone who may have fallen away or backslidden. When we are soaring with the Lord we are seen as healthy and doing great in the eyes of other believers and God.

My heart is that I may have challenged some of us to say, "It's time!" Time to start stepping it up and treat our body with the same discipline that we treat our soul.

The body is indeed temporary and the soul is more important, but that does not mean we should ignore the importance to having an outward witness of Jesus that can be seen by people just looking at us!

BIG IDEA:

Maintaining our physical health through a healthy diet and exercise is part of being all God created us to be. We can all find ways in our lives to grow in this area as we strive to care for God's temple, our bodies.

GROUP STUDY QUESTIONS:

1. How is eating healthy and exercising part of our spiritual lives?

2. Do you keep track of your calorie intake or limit your food intake?

3. What is your biggest struggle with developing an exercise routine?

4. How can you put exercising into your schedule?

5. After reading this chapter, what is one thing you will put into practice or one thing you will change in your life?

6. How can we, as a group, help you do this?

SECTION 4:
Roofing:
Building A
Covering For
Your Family

18

COMMITTED TO STAY

By: John Lanza

As a young boy growing up, I can remember having a tendency to constantly run away. This happened mostly on Saturdays.

It wasn't because I had terrible parents, just the opposite. I was raised in a great home by parents who provided everything I needed to be a well-rounded person. They loved God and went to church each week, taking their four children with them.

As I look back now as an adult, father of three with three grandchildren, I have come to the conclusion that it must have been my issues. I didn't want to be accountable to the responsibilities I had to my family, which, as an elementary age person, weren't many.

As a young boy, I viewed the world and everything in it as supporting my happiness. When that wasn't the case, well, you know, "It's always easier to blame someone else, other than yourself."

Often when I felt like running away, I just picked up my marbles, (actually it was a James Bond lunchbox filled with a thermos of juice and some snacks) and took off up the street. I got as far as a block away, perching myself under my third grade teacher's maple tree.

After working through my issues of self pity and frustration, I headed back home within the hour.

Guys, it's easy to pack your lunchbox and run away. I'm not saying the decision is easy, but the temptation to do so is emotionally appealing. During a day when your current life situation isn't making you happy, we live in a culture that says, "You have every right to run and look for a new place of happiness."

But so often you learn, as I did, home was the right place for me.

I think of the "Prodigal Son," a story I believe most every adult recognizes, like David and Goliath or Jonah and the Whale. The Prodigal Son is frustrated, and he wanted to cut ties with the family. He wants to explore everything he feels he is not getting from his homestead.

His father grants him permission and off he goes with all of his spoils. He made new friends, tasted of the carefree and wild life until his source ran out. With none of his new companions around and unable to buy any more of his new happiness, he had an "under the maple tree" moment that brought him to his senses. He said:

> *All those farmhands working for my father sit down to three meals a day, and here I am starving to death. I'm going back to my father. I'll say to him, "Father, I've sinned against God, I've sinned before you; I don't deserve to be called your son. Take me on as a hired hand. He got right up and went home to his father."* (Luke 15:17-20, The Message)

Andy Andrews made this statement, "When confronted with a challenge, the committed heart will search for a solution, the undecided heart will search for an escape."[1]

The grass always seems greener on the other side...until you get there.

A few years ago, I personally went through some of the most challenging times in my life. I was confronted by misrepresentations, personal attack on my family and myself, all while doing something I knew I was called by God to do---serve the world.

It was at that time I discovered a whole new level of emotions. Not all of them were healthy; many of them left me wanting to "search for an escape."

I found myself searching the want ads on the internet, looking for another position than what I was doing then. Even being a greeter at Walmart was appealing. (No disrespect intended.)

My point in sharing all of that is, although I wanted to escape, God had a different plan, and I committed to stay.

That wasn't an easy decision to reach as I looked at the love of my life struggling every day to heal from the hurt she incurred; as I watched her work through the emotions a wife and a mother feel when her cubs and papa bear are threatened. What brought us through then, brings us through now, and I am sure it always will: the truth that God is committed to His beloved.

The writer of the Book of Hebrews ends with these words of encouragement,:

> *May He equip you with all you need for doing his will.* (Hebrews 13:21, NLT)

I would remove the word "may" and add "will"… He WILL equip you.

For someone who has walked with the Lord for a number of years, like many, I knew that the Lord was with me in those times; He always has been since we've begun this journey together. However, because of that difficult time, I know Him, I know His ways, and I know how He equips, unlike I knew before this time.

All because His voice inside said to me, "Stay."

When you commit to staying, you will experience change.

I can't promise you that change will always be positive from a situational perspective, but when you commit to staying, and that commitment is based on a decision to honor and obey God, what you will experience is a move from the dark side of hopelessness to the bright side of hopefulness.

That hopefulness will energize your confidence that nothing is impossible with God. (Luke 1:37)

Hopefulness has a way of clearing up the murkiness that distorts our ability to see clearly. Hopefulness washes away all the elements that negativity and defeat awaken, by renewing our minds, the way that we think, through the cleansing of God's Word. (Ephesians 5:26)

The change will more likely be happening on the inside of you, before you see it happening in your situation. Yet, like the prodigal and myself, it's better to be at home.

I would be remised if I did not bring into this chapter the time Moses, Aaron and Hur stood atop the mountain as the Israelites did battle with the Amalekites. (Exodus 17:10-13)

As long as Moses raised his staff towards the heavens, the Israelites were winning the battle, but all of us know we have physical limitations. As the battle was a long one, Moses would get weary, and his arms would want to collapse.

To assure a victory, Aaron and Hur would come alongside of Moses and assist him during those moments of weakness. Can you see where I am going with this?

Whenever we have made a commitment, whether it is to people or a situation, there will be times we will have to do battle to stay true to our commitment and honor our word. Like Moses, we will need an Aaron and a Hur to come alongside and assist us into victory.

Be prepared: Sometimes assistance comes in the form of tough love, confrontation, and intervention - ways that may seem painful and inappropriate at the time. But when spoken and handled in love, even these can be very timely.

Something I have found that works in every situation is an attitude to serve. I really believe this applies to the idea of staying, also.

Here's what I mean:

If we can focus on the needs of others and how we can contribute to meeting those needs, it will create an opportunity for God to refresh us.

Let me cite one more factual story from the Bible that illustrates this point. It's the story of Elisha and the woman from Shumen.

This wealthy woman invited Elisha to her home to have a meal with her and her husband. Every time Elisha came to town, she would do this. It happened so often that they decided to build a room onto their house for him. This is how they served him.

Hoping to repay her kindness, Elisha asked if there was anything he could do for her. She was unable to have children, so Elisha prayed. The next year when he visited, Elisha met her baby boy.

Sadly, a few years later, while he was still very young, the boy took ill and died.

Elisha again took this matter to God, and God restored the boy to life. This is how Elisha refreshed a desperate couple in need.

Another way to look at it....

> *The generous will prosper; those who refresh others will themselves be refreshed.* (Proverbs 11:25, NIV)

When I think of this woman and her husband facing the death of their son, I think of all the raw emotion that must have been present. They must have had a strong desire to get out from underneath the weight of that pressure. I'm sure they felt the need to find an escape to a happier place, but look what they would have missed seeing----a lifetime given back to their son.

I have a good friend who is in the construction business. We were having a discussion one day, and he was telling me about a job he is pricing out. As I listened to him, I was amazed at how much time he was putting in just to present and prepare with the folks he was going to build the home for.

So I asked him, "Why so much time?"

His response made very reasonable sense, "If I don't make the investment of time now, it will cost me and the homeowner more later."

A commitment to stay is a long-time investment. It is something you must pour yourself into.

Be patient, keep choosing to stay, and you will enjoy the dividends of that investment.

BIG IDEA:

Often times, the trials of life tempt us to walk away and give up. Yet a true man of God is committed to staying, overcoming the obstacles and fighting for the things that are dear to him in life.

You have heard it said before, "Anything worth having is worth fighting for." That's how God felt about mankind, and I for one am glad He did. As men of God, we are to follow His example and be men who stay.

GROUP STUDY QUESTIONS:

1. Have you ever thought about escaping? If so why?

2. What can you do today that will shut the door on escaping?

3. Who might be your Aaron or Hur?

4. Men carry a lot of pride; is this an issue that will prevent you from reaching out to others?

5. Who might you be able to become an Elisha to today and serve?

6. After reading this chapter, what is one thing you will put into practice or one thing you will change in your life?

7. How can we, as a group, help you do this?

19

BEING A GODLY HUSBAND

By: Roland G. Coon

When we think of building a house, we place great emphasis upon a strong foundation, which definitely makes sense for a stable structure. However, many times the roof is not given priority even though it too gives stability for the walls and is a covering from the elements.

If we don't have a sturdy roof covering the building, the weather will pour in, bringing decay and destruction to our investment. It may happen little by little with water damage, black mold, and rotting wood, but eventually it will cause enough damage that it will require a major overhaul and investment of money.

Therefore, the roof is as important as the foundation. In the same way, a godly husband is a covering over his marriage and family. It's important to understand what being that covering means.

Ephesians 5:20-33 captures this beautiful picture of Christ and His bride. Take a close look at verses 25-28 as written in the Message:

> *Husbands, go all out in your love for your wives, exactly as Christ did for the church—a love marked by giving, not getting.*

Christ's love makes the church whole. His words evoke her beauty. Everything he does and says is designed to bring the best out of her, dressing her in dazzling white silk, radiant with holiness.

And that is how husbands ought to love their wives. They're really doing themselves a favor—since they're already "one" in marriage.

These verses suggest that just as Christ is head of the church and takes care of it by giving up His life to make her clean and holy, so the husband's responsibility to his wife is to love her so deeply that he is giving up his life (denying to self daily) to nurture and protect her.

Our leadership is not in demanding, but in sacrificing and giving out of love, just as Jesus did.

It was said of Jesus that He *"came not to be served but to serve..."* (Mark 10:45) We lead by serving as godly examples as we internalize the Word of God into our everyday lives and relationship with our wives.

When counseling marriages in my earlier years, I would come home and say, "Honey, I owe you an apology."

With a high-pitched voice, she would say, "Oh, really?"

Of course, she wanted to know what I meant.

While guiding a young husband to be more loving, forgiving, and helpful with his wife, I would begin to feel convicted. I wasn't a terrible husband; I just realized that there was room for improvement in applying the Word of God in my own relationship with my wife.

I made a promise to my wife before God on my wedding night: "For better or for worse, for richer or poorer, in sickness and in health." This meant that I had a responsibility to do the right thing before the Lord, as Christ did and does for the church today.

I did not marry my beautiful wife to have her take care of me, but to allow her to become all that God made her to be as a woman, wife, mother, and co-pastor in the work of Christ.

I recall times when my wife was trying to invest in me and help me, but I would give her a hard time. One reason I later learned was that my insecurities were so deep. I thought she was being critical and attacking me. I felt like a failure as a husband and leader. I would become defensive instead of receptive, angry instead of appreciative of her feedback.

However, what she was really doing was caring enough that I become a better man, Christian, husband, Dad, and pastor. Over time as I surrendered to the truth of the Word of God and honestly desired to be a godly man and husband, God healed me of my insecurities. It was then that I found my security in God, not what others thought of me. Then I was able to see her loving, honest feedback for what it was.

I resolved to become a better man in what I call the five worlds of mankind: Being a better Christian, husband, dad, hard worker/provider which sums up into number five, being a godly man.

To become this man, it required that I pursue God. I pursued God through Bible study, prayer, meditation, and just as importantly, practicing what I learned.

Some of you are thinking, "Well, you're a pastor; you have to do those things."

Yes, a pastor should be pursuing God, but I'm first a man who needs transformation. The Word must change me first before I can minister it to others, especially my wife and family.

I remember one time we were supposed to have lunch with a very reputable figure in our community. As a young pastor, I felt the pressure to make sure we were on time. I didn't want to leave a bad first impression since she was very influential.

I went to pick up my wife, and, as I waited for her to come out to the car, I became impatient. I began to honk the horn repeatedly with little time in between; not exactly a Jesus honk!

I was getting perturbed. I waited and waited … and waited, looking at my watch. She finally came out, and the look on her face told me to just be quiet, something I normally would not do. She got in the car and began to explain that a lady from the church had called and she could not get off the phone. Wow, was I ever glad I kept my mouth shut and finally chose to practice patience!

At the time, I didn't realize what I had chosen to do. However, today I know that I chose to be a spiritual and emotional covering for my wife. Instead of showering words that could have cut and hurt her, I simply listened with an understanding heart.

How did that make her feel? As I shared this later, she admitted she was relieved and grateful since she expected the opposite because of all the previous honking.

Not only did I choose to exercise the fruit of the Spirit called patience, but I was practicing the Scripture:

> *A gentle word turns away wrath, but a harsh word stirs up anger.* (Proverbs 15:1, NIV)

It's not knowing the Word of God that makes us godly; it's practicing it. I have had to practice that particular Scripture many times with many different people, and I know how difficult it can be; but it always works and produces godly results.

We receive our love and nurture from God. We need to be vulnerable before God and pursue His Word and heart so we can pass on the same kind of cherishing that Christ has for us, onto our wives and children.

As a pastor, I pray, seek God, study, and research the Word so I can lead the church I am shepherding. It's really no different as the husband of my wife. I have literally studied the Word and sought God for the wisdom and transformation I need to be the kind of husband I should be. Believe me, I have failed many times, but as the years pass, I see where God has helped me to put a roof of protection upon my marriage because I cared to be a covering for my wife and family.

Any unconfessed sin, ungodly habit, immorality, unforgiveness or bitterness leaves a crack through which the enemy can attack or impact my family. But each time I choose to align myself with God's Word, I repair those cracks, bringing godliness to myself and protection to my family.

You put the plywood, the tarpaper and the shingles on top of the house. It represents the knowledge of God, a relationship with Christ and the work of the Holy Spirit within to keep a person strong.

My wife can be as strong as she wants to be in Christ. I can't control that. But how effective she becomes is my part as well. If I choose to be a spiritual husband, it helps protect and support her growth to be a spiritual woman, wife, mother, and minister.

Under this roof, I have to make sure that spiritual activity is going on first for myself and then for my family. While our three children were growing up, I made sure we had devotions five to six times a week. When I took my kids to school, we sang and prayed in the car. We would also sing and pray on the way to church even if we had a difficult start at home. We prayed over them when sick or sad and rejoiced with them in their victories.

My wife and I did not always have devotions together because we did them at different times than each other for years. However, we always checked in on each other and what we were receiving in our times of study. We prayed with and for each other and still do to this day.

Ecclesiastes 4:9-12 (NLT) tells us:

> *Two people are better off than one, for they can help each other succeed. If one person falls, the other can reach out and help. But someone who falls alone is in real trouble. Likewise, two people lying close together can keep each other warm. But how can one be warm alone? A person standing alone can be attacked and defeated, but two can stand back-to-back and conquer. Three are even better, for a triple-braided cord is not easily broken.*

Praying together bonds you together spiritually, creating that protective, three-strand relationship with God against which you cannot be defeated or conquered.

Sometimes verbal prayer is easier for a woman than a man; don't let that intimidate you. You are her spiritual covering and support, and she will cherish your prayers no matter how much you falter at first. It will come more natural over time.

There is a mutual protection when two people pursue God and live out His Word. A healthy spiritual marriage is a protection and defense against harm and destruction for your family. Together, your godliness is your greatest offense against the enemy.

There is a great aggression against our marriages today like never before. We need to pursue godliness as a protection against the one who has come to steal, kill and destroy.

Godliness is God's goal for us as men. We know anything that is His will He will accomplish as we cooperate in the process. God has given us all we need in His Word as building materials for a strong home and family.

May everything we do and say bring out the best in our wives, that she might be dazzling and radiant in holiness, and may our roof be strong and sturdy against all storms.

BIG IDEA:

God has called husbands to be men who allow the Holy Spirit to change us and make us into the man He wants us to be. When we do this, we will become the godly husband that our wives need us to be.

GROUP STUDY QUESTIONS:

1. What does it mean for a husband to be the head of the house?

2. Why do men need to accept correction from our wives? Why do many struggle with this?

3. Why is listening important for a man to be a godly husband?

4. How will being a man committed to Bible reading and prayer make you a better husband?

5. Do you pray with your wife?

6. After reading this chapter, what is one thing you will put into practice or one thing you will change in your life?

7. How can we, as a group, help you do this?

20

BEING A GODLY FATHER TO YOUNG CHILDREN

By: John Knudson

"I don't EVER want to be like him!"

I remember saying this over and over again as a kid.

My dad was an extremely hard worker. He was very serious about providing for his family and making sure that we had everything we needed. (We did not have everything that we wanted, but always what we needed.) In doing so, he was not home very much. He traveled a lot, and we only saw him a couple of evenings a week and on Saturdays.

My dad wasn't really much of a family man. He didn't enjoy getting together with family or relatives. He liked being at home when he wasn't working. He would relax, watch a movie or football game, and do some chores around the house that my mother saved for him.

I remember my dad doing a couple of big projects around the house. He wasn't really into construction or building, but he tried.

One time, in particular, I remember him building a bathroom downstairs. He took a small area in the back corner of our basement living room and built two walls to make the bathroom. Then, he broke through the concrete floor to run the sewer lines out of the house and tied them into the existing ones. He ran all of the water pipes and even installed a shower! I remember thinking throughout this whole process, "Wow! My dad just built a bathroom out of nothing!"

As great as that was, something was missing. While I was able to observe my dad while he built that bathroom, I wasn't allowed to help. I wasn't able to get in there, roll my sleeves up and lend a helping hand. (I was only seven or eight years old, so I don't think I really would have helped all that much, but it was still the point.)

I was told to leave. I was told I wasn't good enough. I was told I couldn't help.

After I got married, my wife and I started our own family. I remember uttering those same words that I did as a kid, "I don't EVER want to be like him!"

I was scared. I was hurt. But this phrase became my passion; my mission. No matter what, I wasn't going to do to my kids what my dad had done to me.

I remember sitting in church one Sunday, listening to the pastor speak from the Old Testament book of Deuteronomy. He was talking about teaching children the way they should go. At one point, the pastor told us that the Bible says that we should be writing down the things of God and talking to our kids, always, about the things of the Lord, and His goodness to us.

Fix these words of mine in your hearts and minds; tie them as symbols on your hands and bind them on your foreheads. Teach them to your children, talking about them when you sit at home and when you walk along the road, when you lie down and when you get up. Write them on the doorframes of your houses and on your gates, so that your days and the days of your children may be many in the land the Lord swore to give your ancestors, as many as the days that the heavens are above the earth.

(Deut. 11:18-21, NIV)

This really intrigued me. I was curious. I was already struggling with how I was going to raise this little boy that God had entrusted to me. I didn't want to mess it up. I didn't want to be like my dad.

In the following days, weeks and months, as I began to think about what that preacher said, I struggled.

I knew what I should do, what I wanted to do, but I didn't know how to do it. I didn't feel like I had an example to look at and see that being modeled.

I knew that I had to raise my children the right way. I was the one (along with my wife, of course) who had to teach, correct, discipline, love, guide and raise this child. This was a pivotal moment for me. To be honest, I knew that I needed to change. I knew that I couldn't continue to do the things that I was currently doing. I wasn't living up to the biblical standards of being a godly father.

I have made a lot of mistakes raising my children. I wish I could tell you something different. I wish I could have been a great example for some other young, struggling dad. But in the early years, I wasn't. I feel like nothing went right. I was missing something. I wasn't including God.

Our family began to grow, and, as it did, my awareness for change grew as well. My wife was always very supportive, even in the dark times, even when I didn't deserve her love and grace and the truth was hard to hear.

I began to get back into God's Word and ask Him to show me what I needed to do.

The Bible says, in 1 Samuel 8:6: *But when they said, "Give us a king to lead us," this displeased Samuel; so he prayed to the Lord.* (NIV)

What great advice!

In this passage, Israel was asking Samuel for a king. Samuel was old and not able to do what he once did. His sons were appointed to help, but were not following the ways of God. The people recognized what was happening, and so they asked Samuel for a king. In Samuel's displeasure, he sought after God.

Guys, that's what you and I need to be doing!

In everything that we are uncertain of, or in the areas that we are just unknowledgeable, we need to seek God and allow Him to guide us.

I believe that is one of the keys to building a covering for your family: Seeking God and allowing Him to guide us.

We don't have to measure up to someone else. Our family doesn't need to "look like" someone else's. My family needs to be the family that God has intended us to be. Your family needs to be the family God has intended it to be. Your family doesn't have to look like mine, and vice versa.

Can you relate?

Is something about fatherhood displeasing to you?

Is there something that is happening within your home that is bothering you?

I would encourage you to seek God, like Samuel did.

If you continue reading through this story, you will see that God calms Samuel and directs him. He shows him exactly what to do. God took care of it for Samuel and He'll take care of it for you, too! Seek the Lord and He will show you what you need to do. He will guide you as you try to implement those processes.

There is another verse of Scripture that has become extremely helpful to me as I journey through my fatherhood adventures.

> But Daniel resolved not to defile himself with the royal food and wine... (Daniel 1:8, NIV)

To resolve means "to decide firmly on a course of action."

Daniel resolved. He decided firmly, that he was going to follow the ways of God and not do what the king was telling him to do. Honoring God and His statutes was more important to Daniel than listening to the king.

I have found in my life that following God and pleasing Him has to be more important to me than following others or doing what they say.

I have to resolve. I have to decide firmly that I am going to raise my kids in the ways of the Lord.

I am going to make it my mission, to teach my kids about Jesus, take them to church, read them the Bible, and everything else that the Lord asks me to do, as their father.

Is it easy? No.

Is it necessary? Yes!

As you and I, as fathers, build a covering for our families, we are also leading by example. Our kids are watching. They are observing. They are listening.

As I began to share the Word with my kids, and I began to lead them by example, I realized that it wasn't as hard as I thought it was going to be.

My kids liked it. They enjoyed it. And, to be honest, when I was too tired or had other things on my mind, they would remind me that we needed to read our Bibles. God has birthed a hunger and passion inside of them, for the things of Himself. Believe me, that's not because I am good or because I have figured out some special formula. It's because I took that first step and decided I would step up and do it God's way and He has honored that.

He is drawing these kids unto Himself. If you will seek Him and lead your kids the way He intends, He'll draw your kids unto Himself as well. It's who He is. It's what He does.

Do you need to resolve that you are going to raise your kids in the ways of the Lord?

Listen, it's not too late. Maybe you're reading this and are thinking, "Man, I've messed this up. I haven't done what the Lord's asking me to do. I blew it. It's too late."

I want to encourage you and let you know that it's not too late!

As long as your kids are still around, even if they've grown up and moved out, it's not too late. God can always use you as a godly figure in the life of your child, no matter how old they are. God is a God Who forgives and forgets! He is a God of second chances...and third... and fourth... and fifth!

Our families need a covering. In the world we live in today, with all of the immorality and ungodliness, we can't afford to expose our families, especially our kids, to the wickedness of this world, without them having this Godly covering. Unfortunately, we can't completely protect them from every bit of wickedness, but we can give them Jesus and His Word, and God will protect them.

Our families need us to be the men, and fathers, that lead them to God.

BIG IDEA:

All of us want to leave a positive legacy. All of us want to build strong, godly coverings over our families and our kids. You can do that! You can be the spiritual head of the house. You can raise your kids up in the ways of the Lord and empower them to live godly lives.

GROUP STUDY QUESTIONS:

1. Are you comfortable with where you are as a father?

2. As a father when you see or hear something that displeases you, how can you respond, following Samuel's model?

3. The Bible says that Daniel resolved to the Lord not to defile himself. In what specific ways can you resolve to be a good father?

4. Is there another godly man that you can confide in? One who can hold you accountable? Or even just ask you every once in a while, "How's it going?" How can you approach him about holding you accountable.

5. After reading this chapter, what is one thing you will put into practice or one thing you will change in your life?

6. How can we, as a group, help you do this?

-21-

FATHERING GODLY TEENS TO GODLY ADULTS

By: Dan Courtney

There is a diner I frequent that has a couple of those famous skyscraper pictures from New York City. You know the ones I'm talking about, where these crazy men are working on I-beams high above the city with apparently no safety precautions whatsoever.

One of my favorites shows eleven men sitting side by side on this I-beam eating their lunch, with massive buildings dwarfed below them in the background. I am not afraid of heights; it's the falling that scares me. Still, I can't help looking at these men and thinking about how one little slip, and their life is over!

Many times I think that raising teens is a lot like what these men faced working on these skyscrapers. It's high risk! We feel like one little mistake, and we'll mess up their lives forever!

We can't get caught up in the thought that one mistake will ruin our sons and daughters. We can't forget that God made kids resilient, so they could rebound from the mistakes of others. Instead of worrying about the "high risk" by trying not to fail, we should seek out the "high rewards" if we raise our kids with the purpose of following the Lord.

Just like the building of that skyscraper, we have the ability to help our teens become adults who will reach heights we never dreamed of! With God's help, we can finish the greatest construction project of our lives: building our kids into godly men and women.

In my twenty-plus years as a pastor, I have seen so many scenarios with young people and families. I've seen godly parents raise kids that leave the church as soon as they are able and abandon their faith altogether. Sometimes these are the kids of Christian leaders or even pastors.

I've seen other kids come from really rough home situations, homes that were even hostile towards Christianity, and yet they sell out completely to Jesus. In spite of great opposition at home, some have even become leaders in the church themselves.

We all know of people who either "beat the odds" and got out of a bad situation to turn out great, or did the opposite, squandering what was seemingly a great upbringing or opportunity. But we need to know that these are outliers, not the norm. More commonly, young people will grow up to be a reflection of their environment in childhood. The seeds that are planted in their lives are the plants that will grow. So we have a choice: We can leave it to chance that our children will beat the odds, or we can proactively plant the seeds that we want to see growing in their lives.

Our children are far too important to leave to chance!

In this chapter, I want to invite you into my office, as I walk myself and other men through a process of doing our best to ensure that our kids grow up loving and serving God. If you are like me... you prefer simple. So here is the process, pillars to build our great skyscraper (our teen into a godly adult), on:

1. Live out your faith

2. Love your wife

3. Love your kids

4. Lift their value

5. Love the results

I believe that if you implement these ideas, your odds of success will be very high. I also want to reach out to those of you who have adult kids already. They are still looking to you for direction. If you will make sure you are doing these things even now, you will still make an impact on them.

So let's get started!

LIVE YOUR FAITH

I cannot overstate this as the cornerstone of this great building project. I heard many years ago that, for many people, their view of God is similar to how they see their own dad. This is scary because none of us are worthy to be compared to God. It most definitely needs to humble us, and cause us to pay attention.

GOD THROUGH MY CHILD'S EYES

If my children see me as intimidating, angry, or crabby, then they may see God that way. If they see me as distant, absent, or unreachable, then they may feel that God is not around either. If we don't have time for them, then God won't either. If we are always seeing the things they do wrong or criticizing them, they might not be able to comprehend the wonderful grace of God, because they see Him waiting for them to make another mistake, too.

On the other hand, if we are loving and caring, then they can see God as loving and caring. If we keep our promises, then God will be trusted to keep His promises, too. If we are happy, joyful, fun...if we are calm, peaceful, patient...if we are gentle, kind, and complimentary...then we open up an easier path for them to see these great qualities in God, too.

Here's the key: We can't possibly represent God well, unless our own faith is real. Paul wrote to the people he was leading in Corinth:

> *...you should imitate me, just as I imitate Christ.*
> (I Corinthians 11:1, NLT)

185

We need to be able to say this to our teens, because whether we believe it or not, our kids will imitate us.

What does it mean to live out my faith?

Faith in God is a journey, an adventure. It has ups and downs, twists and turns, victories and failures. There is so much we must learn as we go. And it is that learning that is the living out of our faith.

LEARN AS YOU GO

We learn best when we put our faith to the test. If we are looking, we'll see that God sends opportunities our way that will test our faith all the time. Our family has even learned to pray over the little things: lost keys, lost phone, something doesn't work, we need to get an appointment but the doctor is booked up, etc.

Just yesterday as I wrote this, I was driving home for Wednesday night Youth Group, about a twenty-five minutes drive from where I was. I was at a place where I could have literally taken either leg of a fork in the road, and they would be about the same distance and time. I actually prayed about which way I should take, and felt a clear direction on it. The awesome thing was that halfway home on that road, one of my staff members was broken down. There they were, on the side of the road, phone in hand, getting ready to call me.

You would not believe how often things like this happen when we really do put our trust in God. I shared this story with many people, especially my teenage daughter, because it is an example of living out my faith.

That is an easy part of living out my faith. It's not so easy when you are mad about something, and feel justified in your anger. That is where it gets hard. When our emotions are charged over something, it is easier to take matters into our own hands than it is to turn it over to God and trust Him. We need to know that our teens are watching closely in those times. They want to know how to handle such things in their own lives. So they are tuned in.

We have two opportunities to live out our faith in these situations. We can handle it right the first time by taking our concerns to God and allowing Him to lead us through it without doing something we should not do. Or if we didn't handle it right, we must own up to that; we must be humble enough to do this in front of our kids.

This is a powerful way of living out our faith, because it helps us grow through proper humility. And when our kids see their strong dad being humble, it has a great impact on them. They will grow too, and it will help them to understand that true humility is a strength and not a weakness.

LIFE IS FULL OF CHALLENGES

Living out your faith allows you to show your kids how to take on challenges as a believer. Allowing God to lead you through those challenges, and letting your kids see you do it, will empower them to do the same. We can't say to our kids, "Do as I say, not as I do."

As dads, often we don't have to say it with our mouths, because our actions may say it for us. In fact, many times our teenage son or daughter will not hear any of the words we try to tell them unless they match up with the life we are actually living out in front of them.

Perhaps the greatest form of living out our faith is when we lead others to Jesus. As a dad, perhaps the greatest thing you could ever accomplish in life is to lead your son or daughter into a born-again relationship with Jesus.

Don't leave this to someone else. There is no more important thing we can do for our kids, and there is no more rewarding thing we can do in our life, than to lead our children into a life-giving relationship with Jesus. Then teach them what it means to follow Him, simply by living out our own faith in front of them, beside them, and right along with them.

LOVE YOUR WIFE

Trying to keep things in the right order, loving your wife is the second pillar because it is the greatest example of love your teen has (good or bad), and it can become a great source of security for them if we do it right. They learn a lot from movies, TV, music, and their friends, but that is NOT where we want them to learn about love or family.

Let me state here that many parents get this one wrong. Far too often, parents will put their children's needs above their marriage relationship. The problem is that their greatest need after Jesus is for their parents to have a strong marriage.

We want to value our kids, which I'll talk about later, but a shaky marriage is not going to help them in any way. I've never heard of a case where children were neglected because the husband and wife were paying too much attention to each other or because all they worried about was the marriage and they forgot about the kids. It just doesn't happen. When the marriage relationship is strong, the family is strong, and the kids are healthy. When the marriage relationship is weak, the family falls apart, and kids become angry and bitter. It is anything but healthy.

I am a very passionate person, and so is my wife. When we have "disagreements," it can get crazy. There is a tension in the home that everyone can feel. Sometimes voices get raised... okay...we yell at each other!!! And we have even been known to get in each other's faces or run out of the room. (Yeah, I know we're the only ones that carry on like that sometimes.) Still, our kids see that. They know when mom and dad are fighting, and they hate it. When that happens, we both know how critical it is for us to get past the issue, make up well, and for them to know that we made up.

This is part of real life. Disagreements happen.

Sometimes my wife and I handle them well; many times we don't. We both know there are certain lines we won't cross. We never lay a hand on each other, and we have gotten better through the years at not pulling out word weapons on each other. Still, we've had some doozies.

Unfortunately, every time our kids have become scared or insecure, they needed to see very clearly that we made up. More than that, they needed to see that our love for each other was strong and would not give up because we had a fight. They just want to know everything is going to be okay.

Peter wrote some great advice for us:

> *Most important of all, continue to show deep love for each other, for love covers a multitude of sins.* (1 Peter 4:8, NLT)

Not only does God have grace for us, so do our children when we give them the chance. As they exercise that grace towards us, their own faith is growing. It all happens when we come to them in humility, living out our faith.

One last note here: Men, NEVER throw your wife under the bus in front of your kids.

Not every "disagreement" is your fault, but it doesn't matter. Your kids don't need you to tell them who was right; they need to see you love, respect, and honor their mom.

If you lift yourself up, you will go down in their eyes. If you protect yourself, it will be to sacrifice your wife, and sacrifice them. They don't need a dad that is right; they need the security of a dad that loves their mom.

LOVE YOUR KIDS

Loving your kids is the third pillar, even though it is usually vying for the #1 spot on this list. The problem with this pillar is that if you put it first, you will find that the first two I listed never get put in at all.

This third pillar has the ability to completely crowd the other two out because of the sheer time and energy it will demand. However, if we have the first two pillars in place, we have made our own faith top priority in our life and made our relationship with our wife of utmost importance, now we can confidently place the third pillar: loving our kids.

To quote one of my college professors, "Kids spell love T-I-M-E."

This is true with kids of all ages. When our kids become teens, they don't follow you around begging for your time anymore. Now you have to pursue their time, and it can be hard to break into their schedule, but we need to do it.

Some things used to be a given, but are more of a challenge these days.

SPENDING TIME TOGETHER AS A FAMILY

If you're not intentional, it won't happen, and before you know it, they'll be all grown up.

EAT DINNER TOGETHER MOST EVENINGS

We have had a family meeting in the mornings before school that helped us all know what was happening that evening. We've had Sunday evening meetings to map out the coming week. Communicating is important, and doing life together is too. Both of these get harder as your kids get older. So build in some good habits and adapt them as you go to keep them relevant.

1-ON-1 TIME WITH YOUR TEEN

The 1-on-1 time that you need to have with your teen should be both intentional and spontaneous. You want to have fun with them doing some things that were not planned at all, but you also want them to know they are important enough for you to actually plan certain things into your schedule that are just for them.

MAKE A FEW MINUTES FOR THEM AT THE START OR END OF THEIR DAY

It is so simple. I want to make sure I say goodnight to my daughters every night that I can, and tell them that I love them. I can't say it enough.

This is also a great time to pray with them and for them.

This brings a great sense of security while at the same time is teaching them to start and end their day with prayer. It is easy to not find time during the day to pray, but I've built in that habit of starting and ending their day with prayer.

This is also a great time to listen to them.

We need to do this if we ever want them to listen to us. And I have found that bedtime is a time when they will share things they just won't share during the day. Take the time...you won't regret it!

DATE NIGHT

One more intentional thing you can do is to take your teens on dates. It is a little hard to do this if you didn't do it when they were younger, but even if you didn't, start doing it now! I have girls, so the term date works just fine. If you have boys, you don't have to use that term, but you need to spend intentional time with them.

This is the time when two things happen:

First, you can just get to know one another, and catch up on life. As busy as we are these days, that won't happen unless we take time out to make it happen. A date is a great way to do this.

Second, this is the chance to talk about relationships... specifically, what a healthy relationship should look like. If you have a son, you are teaching him how to treat a lady, how to honor her, and how to honor God as he is with her. If you have a daughter, you are showing her how a man should treat her, you are honoring her, and you are honoring God while you're with her.

I have two daughters and we go on dates once a month. Here's a warning: it's far too easy for us to miss a month in our busy lives without realizing it. That's why it's great if your wife helps you be consistent with it.

My two daughters are very different. My older daughter is very spontaneous, and loves to go to new places every time we go out. We explore, and have fun doing that. My younger daughter and I go to the same restaurant every time, Chili's. And she even orders the same thing on every date, kids Mac-n-Cheese. She's 17 now...but this is still her standard order, and we have a great time!

You would not believe how much they open up to me when I take them out like this. We are able to discuss things that I just can't get them to talk about any other time. Of course, these types of conversations are not even possible if one or both of you are on your phones. Put the phones away. Leave them in the car if you have to. These relationships are important enough for you to do everything it takes to get a true one-on-one. So ditch the phones, you will not regret it!

Our dates vary a bit from date to date. Some are very casual, although never too casual unless we're going hiking or something like that. Once in a while, we'll dress up really nice and I will purchase a rose. Sometimes I'll write a card or even a full letter to her. I always get her car door, and I treat her like a real lady...because she is! All the while I am showing her, and talking to her, about how she deserves to be treated.

Yes, sometimes it is awkward. Still these are things that she needs to learn from her dad, so she won't be taken advantage of by some punk!

If this all sounds like a lot of time, you are right. It is definitely a commitment that you will need to make. You're going to have to decide to put down your remote control, your phone, your computer or tablet, turn off the game or the video games, but it's important because once your teens are fully grown, it will be too late. You'll never be able to get that time back! So do it now. Make the decision to give them quality time, and lots of it. It's a decision you'll never regret!

LOVE REQUIRES TRUST

In addition to our time, love is expressed to them when we are willing to admit our faults to them. When we genuinely apologize to them, they see a side of us that earns trust. Real trust is invaluable!

When I told my daughters about writing this chapter, I asked them if there was something in particular that they were thankful for that I did as their dad. They both said, "No...not really."

Okay, I'm kidding. But let's face it, parenting is very humbling at times. Actually, my oldest daughter said something that I didn't expect. She said that one of the things that meant the most to her was that whenever mom and I would fight and make up, I would always come to them and apologize, and make sure they were okay. She said that really helped restore any trust that may have been damaged because of the fight.

This is what I mean about being vulnerable with our kids. I can assure you, since my wife is not watching me write this, that every fight was not my fault. But regardless of who I thought was at fault, I would always go to them after and apologize that it happened, assure them that we worked it through, and tell them that I love their mom and I am committed to her. This gave them a sense of security that can be easily shaken in turbulent times. I know my role as a dad is to help make my kids feel secure, and being vulnerable at the right times is key to this.

***Special thanks to my wife on this one. Many times we both go and apologize together, and there have been times she's encouraged me to go to them. Thanks Jen!

LIFTING THEIR VALUE

As a fourth pillar, lifting or raising the value of our teen, seems to flow closely with the last one, but really is an element all its own that men need to put in place. Nobody can determine a young person's worth like their dad. You have a voice and a platform in their lives that no one else has. If you beat them down with your words, they will live beaten down. If you build them up with your words, they will be able to soar. So how do we get really good at lifting their value?

SHOW AND TELL

Show them they are valuable by valuing them. The things in the last section will definitely do this. Prioritizing time for them shows them they are valuable.

I said I would talk more about the dating piece here. One of the primary purposes of me taking my daughters on dates is to help them see their value. I tell them that they are the only ones that can set their price-tag...which is the price that a man will pay for them.

Here's what I mean: If you sit in the car until a man opens the door to let you out, you have set a price. He then determines whether or not he will pay that price.

If he comes to pick you up and he pulls up to the house and honks the horn, you are setting a price by choosing to run out to his car or encouraging him to come to the door to get you.

My daughter is not a used junker that you get at the "buy here, pay here…bad credit, no problem" lot. My daughter is more likely to be found at the Mercedes Dealership, the one on the showroom that very few people even think about buying because it is so nice! I want her to set her price so high, that by the time someone steps up to pay the price, she knows she's found a winner.

Far too many women have settled for posers. Too many women are abused by men physically, sexually, verbally, emotionally and more.

If men would just value their daughters enough that their daughters would value themselves, then any raggedy guy would not do. The value you place on your daughter can make a huge difference in her life.

If you have a son, teach him to value women and not to settle for women who do not value themselves. Show him by loving your wife and valuing her.

I have bought both of my daughter's purity rings and given them these rings on one of our special dates. They did a similar thing in the movie *Courageous*. I did this to be able to explain their value and talk through what it means to remain pure, but I also did it as a show of value.

It is a nice ring; I paid a good price for it. It is not junk…and neither is she. That's why I write them notes or letters from time to time, to give them a hard copy of their worth, their value. You cannot overdo this.

I want my daughter to grow up loving Jesus, following Jesus, and marrying a man who also loves Jesus and follows Jesus. I want him to work hard, love his family, and be well respected. If I invest these things into my teens, I'll have a great chance of seeing this come true.

TELL THEM THEY ARE VALUABLE

Do this by saying the little words that mean so much:

"I love you, I appreciate you, you're smart, you're cute, you're beautiful, you're a good guy, you're such a gentleman, I am proud of you, I'm thankful for you, or I am so glad you are my son/daughter."

Make your own list.

The power of words to build up or tear down is very real. For every time you say something that tears them down, it will take about 20 times of building them up to make up for it. They cannot hear too much of this from you as their dad. So get started and don't ever stop.

When it comes to sons, a dad must be there. He needs to pay attention to his son and look for the moments where he can assure him that he does have what it takes. He must know that Dad is proud of him and that Dad believes in him.

Likewise, a dad must build a security into his daughter that she is worth fighting for. Beauty is inside and out, and you can build up both of these. You need to be the first guy from whom she hears words of love and acceptance. You make sure she knows she is worth fighting for because she sees you fighting for her.

You do not want her to be swept off her feet by the first guy who knows how to deliver a pick up line. Make sure any young man who wants to pursue her goes through you first. Be that filter for her. When you do this, you're not creating a weak woman, but a strong woman who knows she has great value.

GOD VALUES THEM

Teens today are more insecure than ever, but there are many ways that God values them that can really help. I will highlight a few.

The first of these is the fact that He created them in His image.

This doesn't just apply to Adam and Eve, but all humans:

So God created human beings in his own image. In the image of God he created them; male and female he created them. (Genesis 1:27, NLT)

A second thing they need to know is that He has taken great care to make us perfectly.

The psalmist declares: *You made all the delicate, inner parts of my body and knit me together in my mother's womb.* (Psalms 139:13, NLT)

The prophet Jeremiah wrote: *I knew you before I formed you in your mother's womb.* (Jeremiah 1:5, NLT)

And out of all the things God created in the beginning, after each one we read, "*and God saw that it was good*" (Genesis 1:25, NLT)

But when He created humans we read, *He saw that it was very good!* (Genesis 1:31, NLT).

God values us just as we are!

A third thing that He did to show His value is that He sent His one and only Son, Jesus, to rescue us and restore our relationship with Him.

In the Garden of Eden, Adam and Eve's sin separated them from God, and put the entire human race on a path of separation from God. The Cross at Calvary, that Jesus was crucified on, reunited us with our Heavenly Father.

God went to the greatest lengths to win us back.

In John 3:16, the most memorized verse in the Bible, Jesus said:

For this is how God loved the world: He gave his one and only Son, so that everyone who believes in him will not perish but have eternal life. (NLT)

Jesus also said in John 15:13:

There is no greater love than to lay down one's life for one's friends. (NLT)

Then He did it.

Jesus showed us the greatest act of love in the history of the world by giving Himself completely for us...for your teen...and he/she needs to know that!

LOVE THE RESULTS

When the skyscraper is finished, the view is amazing! It is quite a project to raise a teenager today, but the work is all worth it if you don't stop short.

The truth is, this project is never really finished until you quit investing in your child. They can be fifty years old, but if you are still investing, that building will keep going up, higher and higher. As long as you're investing, you will love the results because they will continually invite you up to see the new view from the increasing heights of their lives. They will be so proud to bring dad in to show off, because it will be safe. And there is nobody in their life that they want to make prouder than you!

> So let's not get tired of doing what is good. At just the right time we will reap a harvest of blessing if we don't give up. (Galatians 6:9, NLT)

None of us can guarantee that our kids will grow up and choose to love and serve the Lord, but if we do our part, I believe the scripture will ring true:

> Direct your children onto the right path, and when they are older, they will not leave it. (Proverbs 22:6, NLT)

BIG IDEA:

With God's help, we can finish the greatest construction project of our lives...helping to build our kids into godly men and women. The five pillars that enable us to do this are:

-Live out your faith

-Love your wife

-Love your kids

-Lift their value

-Love the results

GROUP STUDY QUESTIONS:

1. How is your children's view of God affected by how you live?

2. Why is it important to put your wife before your children?

3. The author stated, "Kids spell love T-I-M-E." What does this mean?

4. What are some ways you can spend more time with your kids?

5. Why should a father apologize to their children when they are wrong?

6. What are some ways you can practice "Show and Tell" with your kids?

7. After reading this chapter, what is one thing you will put into practice or one thing you will change in your life?

8. How can we, as a group, help you do this?

BEING A FATHER TO ADULT CHILDREN

By: KR Mele

When it comes to being a godly father to adult kids, the words that immediately come to mind are: "trust, patience and modeling."

Probably one of the most difficult things that I've had to do in raising my kids is totally releasing them into God's hands. I will be the first to admit that this has been a very difficult transition in my life. If you have children, you will understand what I'm about to describe.

"It's a boy....it's a girl!"

I have had the privilege of hearing both. My son, Luke, was born in 1992 and my daughter, Olivia, in 1995. Upon hearing these words and holding them in my arms in that delivery room, I realized, my life would never be the same.

And then something happened, I blinked and my wife and I were helping them pack up their bags and head out to college. Where did that time go?

TRUST

The first word that comes to mind as we release our kids is "trust."

> *Trust in the Lord with all your heart, and lean not on your own understanding; In all your ways acknowledge Him, And He shall direct your paths.* (Proverbs 3:5- 6, NKJV)

Trust is something that we learn by being placed in situations that make us, well, trust. It's like when you pray for patience, the Lord allows you to be placed in environments that will teach you how to be patient. Fun, huh? So, be careful what you pray for.

I believe that one of the greatest things I'm still learning about being a godly father to adult children is how to completely trust the Lord with them. Because if I "lean on my own understanding," at times my trust would diminish. Let me further explain this a bit.

How many of you that have young adult children have looked at a decision or choice they made and said under your breath, "What are you thinking?" Maybe you even verbalized it to them, and that didn't go over too well.

I'm encouraged by a fact I read that says the frontal lobe of the brain does not fully develop in its entirety until the early to mid twenties!

Studies have shown that this part of the brain controls skills such as problem solving, organized and logical thinking, decision making, impulse control, memory, judgment, social and sexual behavior. So when you're young adult child makes a decision, acts in a certain way or forgets something that you asked them to do, and you yell in frustration, "What were you thinking?" chances are, maybe they weren't thinking at all. (Good thing this is a man's book, because if you're married, our wives may get a copy of this and think this still applies to us as well!)

So, my thought would be, at this point in our child's life, it is vitally important that they grasp this about themselves and begin to train themselves in the way the Apostle Paul shares with us from 2 Corinthians 10:5:

Bringing every thought into captivity to the obedience of Christ. (NKJV)

I've found that at this stage of my children's lives, ages twenty-one and twenty-four, my "trust in the Lord" has increased greatly because now they are out of my hands and placed into His. When they were little, Gina and I pretty much controlled their lives. We were in charge of what they ate, watched, listened to, read…where we went on vacation, making sure they read their Bibles each day, and on and on. We took to heart the verse in Proverbs 22:6 that reminds us to:

Train up a child in the way he should go, And when he is old he will not depart from it. (NKJV)

At this point, it's simply time to put our faith into action by trusting Him with their lives. Whether we realize it or not, the Lord loves our children even more than we do, and we can trust Him with their lives. Continue to pray and place your adult children into His hands.

PATIENCE

The second word is patience. I don't think I need to explain this one too much because it simply goes hand in hand with trust. But patience is such a hard thing to learn. I think that is one reason that God gave us children.

How many of you, when your children were little, kept asking the same questions over and over again? Simple questions like, "Why is the sky blue?" or "How do birds fly?"

Dads, let's be patient with our children---not only when they are little and just learning about life, but also when they begin life outside the walls of our homes and are just starting to figure out life on their own.

It can be a scary time for them. They have so many unknowns, so many questions, so many doubts and fears. If you still have small children in the home, the key is that your patience is reflected in your answers to them so that they continue to ask questions of you when they are leaving the home.

Paul places patience in his "Fruit of the Spirit" list in Galatians 5:22, 23:

> *But the fruit of the Spirit is love, joy, peace, longsuffering, kindness, goodness, faithfulness, gentleness, self-control.* (NKJV)

Didn't see the word patience? How about longsuffering?

Yes, it may seem that you are "suffering long" when your little tykes are asking "why, why, why" over and over again when they are young. But be patient; the questions tend to become less and less as they get older.

When they are young adult children, may we continue to exhibit that loving patience they so desperately need at this stage in their lives. The questions become more difficult to answer as they grow, but be patient with them. This is an ongoing discipline we need to work at in the lives of our adult children.

MODELING

Third word, modeling. The Apostle Paul penned a verse that to me is very challenging as a father:

> *Imitate me, just as I also imitate Christ.* (1 Corinthians 11:1, NKJV)

Imitation can be a good or a bad thing. There are many "imitation foods" out there that are total frauds. If you Google the words "imitation foods," you will find such titles as "10 Fake Foods You're Probably Eating," "Imitation Crab Isn't Crab At All," and "6 Fake Foods You (Will Wish You Didn't) Have in Your Kitchen."

No one likes a fake, right? I mean, the difference between real crab at the Outer Banks in North Carolina and imitation crab out of a can? Come on!

So when it comes to raising our children, let's be the real thing seven days a week and not just on Sunday mornings. Let's not be a fake; let's be the real deal!

Imitation can be a powerful tool when we model the right things. The Apostle Paul wrote these powerful words to the church in Corinth because they needed to see what it was like to follow Christ. As a spiritual father, Paul was saying to them, "watch how I live, imitate me as I model to you what it means to be a Christ follower."

We, as fathers, have the privilege of saying to our children, *"Imitate me, follow me, as I model Christ before you."*

The fact of the matter is, this is done mostly without words.

I'm not sure how many of you can relate to this, but as a dad, I've been known to put my foot in my mouth and had to go back and apologize to my children. Anyone relate?

But above all else, I've tried with Christ's help (and continue to do so) to model Jesus in my life by my actions.

We've all heard the popular phrase, "Actions speak louder than words." So true in being a godly father to adult children!

To be honest, for eighteen years, they received all the training from God's Word that I could give them. Now as they are adults, I've come to the realization that it's time to continue to model what I've taught them and allow the Lord to do His work by the Holy Spirit.

The one thing I want my children to say of their dad is that, "He lived it! He not only talked about Jesus; he lived Jesus." I believe that as our children see us live and model Jesus before them, the questions will come, and the conversations will be had. So I say to all the dads out there...*"Trust the Lord, be patient, and model Jesus before your children."*

And one day I believe we will hear the Lord say to us, "Well, done, Dad."

PRAYERS AND SCRIPTURES TO BELIEVE FOR YOUR CHILDREN:

"Lord, place Godly people around them that can influence their lives."

Do not be deceived: Evil company corrupts good habits. (1 Corinthians 15:33, NJKV)

"As our children plan their course, Lord, would you direct their steps..."

A man's heart plans his way, But the Lord directs his steps. (Proverbs 16:9, NKJV)

"Would You give our children servant's hearts that think of others before themselves..."

For even the Son of Man did not come to be served, but to serve, and to give His life a ransom for many. (Mark 10:45, NJKV)

"Lord, give my children hearts that love mercy, walk humbly and do what is pleasing in your eyes..."

And what does the Lord require of you but to do justly, to love mercy, and to walk humbly with your God? (Micah 6:8, NJKV)

"Jesus, give my children a deep desire to follow you wholeheartedly...."

With my whole heart I have sought You; Oh, let me not wander from your commandments. (Psalm 119:10, NJKV)

BIG IDEA:

It can be frustrating and challenging to parent adult children, but they need us the most at this life-forming time in their lives. When it comes to being a godly father to adult kids, the words that immediately come to mind are: "trust, patience and modeling."

GROUP STUDY QUESTIONS:

1. What does it mean to "trust in the Lord" when it comes to your adult children?

2. Why is it hard to practice patience with adult children?

3. The author stated, "When it comes to raising our children, let's be the real thing seven days a week and not just on Sunday mornings." What are ways to apply this to our lives?

4. What spoke to you the most in this chapter?

5. After reading this chapter, what is one thing you will put into practice or one thing you will change in your life?

6. How can we, as a group, help you do this?

Part 5
Wiring:
Connecting to
the Power
Source

-23-

THE HOLY SPIRIT: GOD'S BUILDING

INSPECTOR

By: Wayde Wilson

God's house is not a building with a steeple. It's people! The Bible says YOU are God's house:

> You are being made into a place where God lives through the Spirit. (Ephesians 2:22, ERV)

> You yourselves are God's temple. God's Spirit lives in you. (1 Corinthians 3:16-17, ERV)

God wants to live inside you. But before He can move in, there's some work that needs to be done to get the place in shape. One of the Holy Spirit's jobs is to get your 'house' ready!

Think of the Holy Spirit as "God's supernatural Building Inspector".

A building inspector is *"a person employed by either a city, township, or county and is usually certified in one or more disciplines qualifying them to make professional judgment about whether a building meets building code requirements. Building inspectors have the power to halt construction work on a site if it does not meet the prescribed standards."*

Some guys in the construction industry don't have a very high view of building inspectors. However, the job of a building inspector is ultimately very important: to make sure the structure being built is safe so people don't get hurt, or even killed by accident. In a similar way, the Holy Spirit wants to work with you to make your 'house' a place where God feels at home. Like the Under Armor slogan, He'll help you "Protect This House."

God doesn't want you to get hurt, and your eternal life is at stake! So let me give you some tips on how the Holy Spirit operates. Although there are several things that go into building a safe, secure structure, the focus of this section of the book is on wiring. Let's start by explaining how the Holy Spirit can help you get the power and lights on in your house.

A LIGHT IN DARK PLACES

"We Bring Good Things to Life" was an advertising slogan used by General Electric between 1979 and 2003. The extremely successful slogan was responsible for increased popularity and a new image for the company. As one of three directors for GP&L (God's Power & Light Company), the Holy Spirit wants to 'hook you up,' and "Bring Good Things to Life" inside you spiritually. But we've got a problem: without a connection to God, we're all in the dark; cut off from the light of His presence.

Have you ever been to a construction site at night? It's dark, dangerous, and even a little scary. If you're not careful, you can get hurt. That's a great description of life without God. Proverbs 4:19 (NLT) says:

> *...the way of the wicked is like total darkness. They have no idea what they are tumbling over.*

Isaiah describes life without God like this:

> *We long for light but sink into darkness, long for brightness but stumble through the night.* (Isaiah 59:9, the Message)

I've met too many guys that fit those descriptions: Stumbling around in addiction. Staggering through a meaningless life. Like a house before it is wired: dark, powerless, and empty. When we're living in sin with no spiritual light in our 'house,' the conviction of the Holy Spirit functions like a flashlight, lighting a path that can lead us out of the darkness.

The reaction His light creates inside us is called 'conviction.' In simplest terms, conviction is an awareness that we've done something wrong or "a declaration that a person is guilty of an offense."[1] It's important to understand that the Holy Spirit doesn't reveal our guilt to make us feel bad (sin already does that!); He points it out so we can get rid of it!

When you feel conviction, that's the Holy Spirit doing His job. Jesus said:

> *When (the Holy Spirit) comes, he will prove the world to be in the wrong about sin and righteousness and judgment.* (John 16:8, NIV)

It is spiritually and emotionally draining to be weighed down with the guilt of sin – like putting in a hard day of physical labor while carrying a backpack full of bricks! David described it well:

> *My guilt has overwhelmed me like a burden too heavy to bear.* (Psalm 38:4, NIV)

God wants to take that burden off your shoulders! So the Holy Spirit shines a light on your sin and tries to lead you to the only One Who can remove it: Jesus. But the choice to follow Him out of the darkness is completely up to you.

When you feel the conviction of the Holy Spirit, you have two options: resist it or admit it. The first response leaves you in the dark. Coming clean before God leads you out of the darkness and into the light.

It's an amazing feeling to unload the burden of your sins. One moment of honest confession changes everything; *"God, I admit I'm a sinner. Please forgive me."*

That's all it takes. Suddenly the light comes on as God moves into your 'house,' drives away the darkness, and connects you to His life-giving power.

> Ephesians 5:8 NLT says: *Once you were full of darkness, but now you have light from the Lord. So live as people of light!*

BLUEPRINT:

Have you ever experienced the Holy Spirit shining the light of conviction into the darkness of your life? What did it feel like? How did you respond?

If God is 'in your house' (life/heart), stop right now and thank the Holy Spirit for doing His job!

SAFETY PROCEDURES (AVOIDING SHORT-CIRCUITS AND POWER OUTAGES)

After you invite God to move in as Lord of your life, the convicting work of the Holy Spirit shifts somewhat. His job now, as your internal Building Inspector, is to help you 'Protect This House.' Even though you have a direct line to God's Power and Light Company, Satan will keep working every day to try and disrupt the spiritual power flow in your life. But, unlike before, when things were dark and the Holy Spirit was on the outside trying to point you towards God, you now have the advantage of Him living inside you.

Can I give you a piece of advice? Hand Him the keys and give Him access to the whole house! You already know He does good work. So let Him do His job! And He will protect you from short-circuits, power outages, and getting burned by sin. Here's how:

HE'LL HELP YOU REWIRE THE PLACE

Once God moves inside us, the Holy Spirit immediately goes to work, inspecting our 'house.' We start noticing things we didn't notice before.

Some of the things we were doing before God moved in make us feel uncomfortable now. That's the Holy Spirit doing His job, convicting us of things that God doesn't approve of. After all, it's not just your house now; it's His!

One of the best stories I can think of to illustrate this spiritual re-wiring process involves my friend, Tim, who attended a church I used to pastor. Tim, a high school student at the time, was dealing and using drugs.

One Sunday morning, Tim gave his life to Christ. There was an immediate change in Tim. He was on fire for God. He started witnessing to his friends at school. Not long after Tim met Christ, he came to see me. I'll never forget that appointment!

Tim came in my office, sat down with a big grin on his face and said, "So Pastor, now that I'm a Christian, should I stop smoking weed?"

I had not preached a sermon on the evils of smoking marijuana. No one at church had pulled him aside and given him a lecture about using drugs. But the Holy Spirit was already at work in this new believer, showing him that he needed to change out the old wiring so God could continue the work He had started in him. I love that story! And I love Tim – who by the way, went on to become a pastor.

When God's Building Inspector convicts you of something, make that change – even if it's hard. Old habits, hangouts, and friends may need to go. Don't take shortcuts that will cost you later! Let the Holy Spirit help you get all your spiritual wiring up to 'code' so you don't lose power or get burned by sin.

INSTALL SAFETY FEATURES

In addition to checking the wiring, a good building inspector will also make sure certain safety features are installed in the electrical system to protect a house. Breakers and GFCI (ground fault circuit interrupter) outlets are designed to shut off the flow of electricity when there is an unusual power surge in order to prevent electrical shock or damage. High-tech cameras are also used to perform infrared scans of electrical panels, components, and wiring; identifying 'hot spots' in the system and providing early detection of problems.

The conviction of the Holy Spirit operates like these safety features, giving us early warning of danger and potential damage that's coming if we continue down paths of compromise. Like a spiritual infrared scanner, the Holy Spirit sees sinful 'hot spots' we try to hide. Knowing this, David welcomed the Holy Spirit to scan his heart often:

> *Search me, O God, and know my heart; test me and know my anxious thoughts. Point out anything in me that offends You, and lead me along the path of everlasting life.* (Psalm 139:23-24 NIV)

If you ignore His early warning signals, the Holy Spirit will trip breakers in your life, trying to stop you before someone gets hurt or the damage is irreversible. I encourage you, like David, to invite the Holy Spirit to search your 'house' every day.

BLUEPRINT:

Have you been putting off re-wiring your 'house' or ignoring early warning signals and blown breakers in your life? Where? How? Let the Holy Spirit help you bring your life 'up to code' before damage takes place!

CODE VIOLATIONS

Two very negative things happen when we ignore the conviction of the Holy Spirit and violate God's Code. Both result in pain that God wants to help you avoid. They are *painful penalties* and *catastrophic loss*.

PAINFUL PENALTIES

Sin eventually hurts us. Every time. So God, Who hates to see us in pain, sent His Holy Spirit to lead us out of sin and provide an internal warning system to protect us. But, unlike an earthly building inspector, God's Building Inspector will not force you to comply with God's 'codes' (standards), or fine you for violations. He will faithfully warn you and point you in the right direction , but the choice to obey is up to you. And if you choose to sin, your sin always writes its own fine.

For Christ-followers, some of the pain of our sin is that it slows or shuts down our spiritual growth and disrupts God's plans for our lives.

The last part of the definition I shared earlier reads, "*Building inspectors have the power to halt construction work on a site if it does not meet the prescribed standards.*" Again, unlike earthly building inspectors, God's Building Inspector won't halt God's work in your life; but sin will. So, if you don't want to look back with regrets over precious time and opportunities lost, listen to and obey the voice of the Holy Spirit!

CATASTROPHIC LOSS

All your life, right up until the moment when you take your last breath, the Holy Spirit will be trying to lead you out of the darkness of sin and into the light of a relationship with God. God only knows how many opportunities you will have to get your spiritual 'house' in order. Dozens – perhaps hundreds of times over the course of your life, you will sense the Holy Spirit doing His job, drawing you to God where you can receive forgiveness. But if you ignore His warnings, you will not only stumble around in the darkness of sin in this life; the Bible says you will live in darkness *forever*.

Jesus described hell, among other things, as a place of "*darkness, where people will cry and grind their teeth with pain*" (see Matthew 8:12 and 22:13 ERV), forever cut off from the presence of God. If you don't like the sound of that, you have one lifetime to respond to God's offer of eternal life. Thousands of people living in the darkness of hell right now would give anything for the chance to trade places with you.

Another form of catastrophic loss regarding the Holy Spirit that often raises questions and concerns is something the Bible describes as "the blasphemy against the Holy Spirit" or "the unpardonable sin." Jesus said, "*...every sin and blasphemy can be forgiven...But whoever blasphemes against the Holy Spirit will never be forgiven; he is guilty of* *an eternal sin.*" (Mark 3:28-29) Those are heavy words.

I've often had people say to me, "How do you know if you committed the unpardonable sin?" or "I think I've committed the unpardonable sin." The simple answer to that question or concern is this: If you still feel the conviction of the Holy Spirit, you haven't committed the unpardonable sin. The fact that you feel remorse or sorrow for your sin tells you that you still care and recognize you have violated God's 'code.'

I don't worry about those who feel the conviction of the Holy Spirit; I worry about those who don't. I often say, "Sin will take you to The Land of I Don't Care."

There isn't a sin that God can't forgive. But there IS a sin that can take us to a place where we no longer care to be forgiven. That sin occurs when someone disrespects the Holy Spirit so deeply that they develop what the Bible describes as a "seared conscience." (1 Timothy 4:2; also Titus 1:15)

Severe burn victims lose the ability to 'feel' when the nerve endings in their body are destroyed. A person who goes so deep into sin that they are willing to disrespect or mock the Holy Spirit is in danger of developing a seared conscience, losing the ability to feel conviction and becoming a permanent resident in "The Land of I Don't Care." So, Paul warns: "*Do not grieve the Holy Spirit.*" (Ephesians 4:30 NIV)

FINAL CONCLUSIONS

I think it's interesting that the Bible refers to the Holy Spirit as a 'gift.' The conviction of the Holy Spirit may make us uncomfortable at times; but He makes us uncomfortable for a good reason. Every time we sense Him trying to lead us out of the darkness or setting off spiritual alarms in our heart we should be thankful. Thankful that we can feel God's presence. Thankful to know that God is trying to help us. Thankful that we are alive and have the opportunity to respond. I leave you with one final blueprint prayer:

BLUEPRINT

"God, thank you for the gift of the Holy Spirit. And Holy Spirit, thank you for the times in my life when You have made me aware of my sin. I know that You only want to help me, so I welcome You to search my heart right now."

Now stop. And listen. If the Holy Spirit makes you aware of something that is out of line in your relationship with God, admit it, ask God to forgive you, and commit to do whatever He tells you to do to 'protect this house' where He lives!

BIG IDEA:

God blessed us with the Holy Spirit Who brings conviction into our lives and helps us overcome sin. He also protects us by warning us not to fall into the enemy's traps. We need to be open and responsive to the Holy Spirit's voice in our lives.

GROUP STUDY QUESTIONS:

1. Why is it important to have the Holy Spirit shining His light of conviction into our lives?

2. How does sin drain us spiritually and emotionally?

3. What is the first time in your life that you remember the Holy Spirit shining His light of conviction into your life?

4. The author stated, "The conviction of the Holy Spirit operates like safety features, giving us early warning of danger and potential damage that's coming if we continue down paths of compromise." What does this mean?

5. What happens when we ignore the Holy Spirit's conviction?

6. After reading this chapter, what is one thing you will put into practice or one thing you will change in your life?

7. How can we, as a group, help you do this?

24

THE HOLY SPIRIT EMPOWERS: CONNECTING TO THE POWER SOURCE

By: Chad Stoecker

Do you know what the difference is between authority and power?

In laymen's terms, authority is the right to achieve, and power is the means to achieve. Authority is usually given through relationship, whereas power is achieved through experience.

Mr. Tyson was my high school history teacher in the Milwaukee suburb where I grew up. He was not from the laid back, Midwestern culture where we lived... he was from west Philadelphia. One day the topic of pranks pulled on rival high schools came up, and he proceeded to tell us what his school did as a "prank" on their rival during a heatedly contested football game.

While the game was being played, they went out to the parking lot and they tipped the visiting team's empty bus on its side. As he broke into hysterics, we all stared at him, frozen in terror until nervous laughs emanated from the group. Mr. Tyson was a teacher that had both authority and power... authority because of his relationship to us, he was an elder and he was a teacher; power because of his experiences and the means with which he communicated. He was my favorite teacher.

One day I showed up to discover we had a substitute. I don't know what got into our class that day, but I realized early on that he had no chance.

Why? Because although he had authority to run the class, he lacked the power to do so, like many substitute teachers.

We had so much fun that day, though short-lived. The next day, Mr. Tyson was back, and he had heard how we treated the substitute. Let's just say, I'm thankful there were no buses.

You may be asking, "What does this story have to do with the power of the Holy Spirit?"

Much like how authority and power go hand-in-hand to be a successful school teacher, supervisor or parent, the same authority plus power is necessary to be an effective man of God.

In Christ's parting words to His disciples in Matthew 28, commonly referred to as "The Great Commission," He says:

> *All authority in heaven and on earth has been given to me.*
> *Therefore go...* (Matthew 28:18-19, NIV).

Christ had authority because His Father had granted Him the authority, and now He was authorizing the disciples and all that would come later (you and me) to reach a lost world with the Gospel.

Jesus Christ also had power because He was God; thus He was able to exhibit all throughout His earthly life the wonderful combination of authority and power.

In this moment, the disciples receive their God-given authority, but what did they lack?

They lacked power. This, I'm afraid, has become a much too usual occurrence: a believer who has accepted the authority salvation affords, but lacks the empowerment of the Holy Spirit.

I have talked with many men who struggle with spiritual confidence, though they have received salvation. I have sat with many men who understand their authoritative role in their home, but struggle to implement any standards. A lot of men understand the authority given in Matthew 28 to reach a lost world, but struggle to talk with their neighbor about Christ.

Why? Just like my substitute teacher, authority without power simply won't get the job done.

For these reasons, the "power" problem is taken care of by the Holy Spirit in Acts 1. Jesus is just moments from ascending to the right hand of His Father, so He instructs them:

> You will receive power when the Holy Spirit comes on you; and you will be my witnesses... (Acts 1:8, NIV)

Within days, a hundred and twenty people go from being "authorized" to reach a lost world to becoming "empowered" to do so.

Let's break it down even more personally...

Do you remember the moment you accepted Christ into your life?

When that moment happened, you stepped into an eternal relationship. You became a child of the living God, a prodigal that had returned not as a servant, but as a son.

When that relationship began you were given the Father's authority. I like how Paul says it to the Roman church:

> Now if we are children, then we are heirs—heirs of God and co-heirs with Christ, if indeed we share in his sufferings in order that we may also share in his glory. (Romans 8:17, NIV)

So your authority was given to you through relationship. Much like the way the disciples were given their authority from Christ on the mountain in Matthew 28, all authority from God the Father given to Christ, was now given to them.

Power, on the other hand, is received through experience.

Do you remember the moment that the Spirit of God became active in your life? When His supernatural power filled you to overflowing, and you just knew something was different?

Most likely this happened as a result of an experience, either at an altar or special service, when you found yourself in the presence of the Lord wanting something more. Much like the Holy Spirit falling on the 120 in the upper room in Acts 2, it was through this wonderful experience that their lives were filled with the Spirit's power.

What has become common in today's busy world is many believers have rested on the authority of their relationship to Christ, but have fallen short in having empowering experiences that come from spending time with Christ. So we boast the authority to win a lost world, we just lack the power to do so.

This is the same power that will give you confidence as a son of God.

This power will enable you to lead your home the way God has designed for you to lead your home.

This is also the power that will give you the wisdom and boldness to reach your neighbor for Christ. This power is available to you right now! So, how do you receive it?

First things first, the Spirit that empowers you is already living within you. When you received the authority of Christ through that saving relationship, the Spirit of God made His home in your spirit. This is where conviction comes from; the Spirit of God prompts your spirit that you are doing something you shouldn't be doing and says "stop it." Conviction is good.

The empowering of the Spirit or "baptism" (flowing over) takes place in your life when you finally allow the Spirit to have total control.

THE DIFFERENCE BETWEEN THE CONVICTING POWER AND THE CONTROLLING POWER OF THE SPIRIT?

If your life were illustrated by you driving an old-fashioned stage coach, the "conviction" of the Holy Spirit would be Him riding shotgun, pointing the way. The "control" of the Holy Spirit happens when you give Him the reins and let Him drive your life.

A great example of this is seen in Peter's life: before Acts 2 he was a man who had "authority" and was able to offer the testimony that Christ was going to build His church on (Matthew 16:18). However, in Acts 2, we see the transformation of a man who has added supernatural power to that authority, and he delivers a message that brings thousands into a relationship with Christ.

This is the life Christ has designed you to live---a life of authority and power.

Don't settle for just a testimony of faith; build on that testimony a portfolio of supernatural experiences.

The world has yet to witness the force that will be exhibited when churches all across our nation are filled with men who have exercised with supernatural power the authority they have been divinely given. Be empowered men!

ACTION POINTS:

TAKE A MOMENT AND INVENTORY YOUR RELATIONSHIP WITH CHRIST.

Are you living with authority, but without power?

Are you willing to have the experiences necessary that will bring about handing over the reins of your life to the Holy Spirit?

SEEK THE SPIRIT'S POWER BY REPENTING OF ANY UN-CONFESSED SINS IN YOUR LIFE.

Pray with desperation and avail yourself to as many opportunities as possible to spend time in the Lord's presence: church services, revival meetings, Bible studies, men's conferences, etc.

REMOVE ALL EXPECTATIONS OF WHAT THE SPIRIT EMPOWERMENT IS TO LOOK AND SOUND LIKE.

Spirit empowerment is a shared experience with the supernatural power of God, not a "to do" list to accomplish. When the Spirit empowers your life, you will know it.

Remember, the power of the Spirit is to embolden the authority of Christ in you. It may come as the result of an experience, but it is to be lived out as a new and empowered lifestyle.

BIG IDEA:

Your wife, children, spiritual brothers and lost neighbors are counting on you becoming empowered. They just may not know it yet. You were created by your Heavenly Father to be a Mr. Tyson, not just a run of the mill substitute. There are lives to rescue, an enemy to defeat, "spiritual" buses to tip over! Let's get busy.

GROUP STUDY QUESTIONS:

1. Why do we need the Holy Spirit to empower us?

2. What is the difference between power and authority?

3. The author stated, "We boast the authority to win a lost world, we just lack the power to do so." What does this mean?

4. How will being empowered by the Holy Spirit help you reach the lost?

5. After reading this chapter, what is one thing you will put into practice or one thing you will change in your life?

6. How can we, as a group, help you do this?

25

BAPTISM IN THE HOLY SPIRIT

By: Bobby Basham

Most construction jobs begin with a dream, a plan, and a building process. The dream is what is wanted or needed. Some dreams are spontaneous while others are thought out over a period of time. A dream can even come by seeing what someone else has built with the realization that it can become our dream as well. Some dreams might even be what we call a "pipe-dream," something that seems so impossible that it could never happen.

However it starts, is not as important as the other two steps.

Once the dream is realized enough to articulate, then the real work begins...the work of putting plans on paper, the job of communicating that dream to the architect who can transfer that dream into a drawing for a builder to construct. Once the plans are drawn and approved by the proper authorities, the contractor can be secured, and the construction can begin.

In considering the baptism in the Holy Spirit for guys like you and me, we often begin with the dreaming process. Let's approach it this way: we need to understand the purpose in order to do the work that achieves the results.

The baptism in the Holy Spirit is the power of God working in and through us to become more than we could ever be without this experience. My own life is a clear example of the reality of the baptism in the Holy Spirit.

I was called by God at an early age to become a minister. Growing up in a pastor's home, I knew exactly what this meant. I can tell you that I was not what anyone would call "preacher material." I was not outgoing! I was a relatively shy boy who was afraid to speak in front of others. I was not the brightest in my classes and better with my hands than with people. I lacked all necessary skills to be an effective communicator for God. But like Paul says in the Bible:

> *Where is the wise person? Where is the teacher of the law? Where is the philosopher of this age? Has not God made foolish the wisdom of the world?* (1 Corinthians 1:20, NIV)

The difference is that God takes the ordinary and makes it extraordinary with the work of the Holy Spirit that overflows in a man's life.

Peter is the best example of the difference made by the baptism in the Holy Spirit, though there are many others. We know him as the outspoken, foot-in-mouth, impetuous guy who caved when the heat was on. We could easily say he choked when he could have been a star. We can't forget that he cursed that he never knew Jesus while Christ was being interrogated. He ran with the others in the Garden of Gethsemane. After Jesus' death, he was cowering in fear, locked in a room for fear of losing his own life.

However, the day of Pentecost came, and the power of God, through the baptism in the Holy Spirit, infused his life with supernatural power. An ordinary fisherman, who had tripped on his own words days earlier, now faced a confused crowd, much larger than the few who had questioned him around the fire barrels in the courtyard, and declared without fear:

This man was handed over to you by God's deliberate plan and foreknowledge; and you, with the help of wicked men, [a] put him to death by nailing him to the cross. (Acts 2:23, NIV)

Then he preached an unprepared sermon spontaneously directed by the work of the Spirit in his life.

From Acts chapter two forward, we see a man on fire for God, doing amazing things that he could never have dreamed about before.

Who could have believed that God could take a fisherman with a limited education and empower him to be a leader in the church? I would urge you to read specifically about his life in Acts, comparing what is written about Peter prior to the Day of Pentecost with what happened on the Day of Pentecost----the inaugural day when the baptism of the Holy Spirit is given to every person who makes themselves available.

THE DREAM

The dream is to be a man empowered by the Holy Spirit to do extraordinary things and also to enhance the skills already in us through God's original design.

The men constructing the first tabernacle in Exodus were:

... filled him with the Spirit of God, with skill, ability and knowledge in all kinds of crafts. (Exodus 31:3, NIV)

Being baptized in the Holy Spirit is a very practical experience in any man's life that enables him to be and do more than could be accomplished without the baptism.

THE PLAN

The Holy Spirit is given to believers by Jesus. After His resurrection in Acts 2, a chapter that I would encourage you to read a few times, there is a pivotal scripture:

The promise is for you and your children and for all who are far off — for all whom the Lord our God will call. (Acts 2:39, NIV)

This reminds us that Jesus is still giving the Holy Spirit to believers. Based on the sequence of Acts 2 and repeated in Acts 8, Acts 9, Acts 19, the people filled with the baptism in the Holy Spirit were people who had come to know Jesus, became believers, and then had another encounter with God, separately, and following the acceptance of Jesus into their lives. They were filled with the Holy Spirit in a manner that was understood by themselves and those around them as being baptized in the Holy Spirit.

Most of us are familiar with being baptized in water. According to the Bible, being baptized in water is when someone is submerged in water, from either standing or sitting in a pool or tank of water, lowered down, and then brought out of the water, illustrating the death, burial and resurrection of Jesus.

The term used in the Bible has specific meaning: "*being fully covered.*" It's interesting that Jesus and the Bible use the same word to describe being what we call, "baptized" in the Holy Spirit.

I observed a speaker illustrate it this way:

He took an empty basin and placed an empty glass in it. He then took a pitcher of water and poured water into the glass; but instead of stopping when the glass was full, he kept pouring water in until the glass overflowed and the water spilled from the glass into the basin.

This is what it means to be "filled to overflow." This is what is meant when the word "baptized" is used to describe the work of the Spirit in a person's life.

The outflow of that experience that has reached the depths of our lives is the words we speak or perhaps the words we can't speak. The work of the Spirit that reaches the overflow level can leave us with a stirring in our lives that we want to express, but can't seem to find the words. This can happen when we are praying and asking God for the gift of the Holy Spirit, or while we are worshiping God for His greatness and for what He has done and continues to do in our lives. When we offer verbal expressions of our love and gratitude for His forgiveness to us and thankfulness for the many times He intervened on our behalf, we can feel or sense His presence; we want to say more.

It is in those moments we can give a voice to the expressions in our hearts that don't seem to have words.

This is talking in a language we are not familiar with or as some call it, "speaking in tongues."

It is not God taking over. It is not about us losing either our consciousness or any of our faculties. Instead, it is about giving a voice of adoration to God who has done so much for us. It is allowing the Holy Spirit to overflow in us, like the glass that is full and then overflowing.

Although one of the desired results of the plan is the overflow of the Spirit, it is not the main focus. Speaking in a foreign language is not the goal. Our desire for the baptism in the Holy Spirit is to allow Jesus to more fully work in our lives, that other people may know Jesus. This has always been the plan of Jesus.

Too often we approach the baptism in the Holy Spirit with ourselves in mind and what benefits we get, when God's concern is for a world to know Him and His love which was demonstrated on the cross through the death and resurrection of Jesus.

Just as a contractor may put much of himself into a custom-home building project, ultimately it is not what he wants that matters. What matters is what the one for whom the home is being built wants.

THE PROCESS

We come to Jesus with a dream, a desire to experience the gift of the Holy Spirit in our lives, so we come asking for the baptism in the Holy Spirit. When we ask Him, we thank Him for this wonderful gift that will enable us to do and to be more than we can do or be on our own.

We worship God with an expectant heart believing God to touch our lives, and, as we worship Him, we sense a stirring in our hearts. We trust a loving God who we know only wants the best for us. He will work in us, and we will, in faith, believe Him and give voice to the work of the Spirit in us that enables the flow of His Spirit out of our lives. This is the plan for the baptism in the Holy Spirit.

Just like with any construction project, there is what is called *normal and customary practices*, meaning there is a particular way we should do things. For example, if we are laying ceramic tile on a wood floor, then a normal and customary building practice would be to first put down concrete backer board in order to install the tile.

A normal and customary plan for receiving the baptism in the Holy Spirit is a surrendered life to God, a desire to have the baptism in the Holy Spirit, and a willingness to talk with God about the receiving of the Holy Spirit through verbal communication. This plan is often combined with worship and the surrender of one's life to Christ.

When Paul questioned the Ephesian believers in Acts 19, he found a small band of dedicated followers doing all they knew; they just didn't know enough. These guys were sincere and teachable. They knew about the ministry of the Holy Spirit through John the Baptist's teaching, but did not know about the baptism in the Holy Spirit which had been experienced by other Christians.

Perhaps that is where you are. You love God and are doing your best to serve Him.

You are doing all you know to do, and now you come to read about the baptism in the Holy Spirit and realize you have not experienced this wonderful work of God in your life.

I want you to know there is more than you have experienced. Like the believers in Ephesus, I believe, if you will pray and ask Christ to baptize you in the Holy Spirit, He will do that.

The Bible reminds us in Luke 11:13:

> *If you then, though you are evil, know how to give good gifts to your children, how much more will your Father in heaven give the Holy Spirit to those who ask him!* (NIV)

You can pray by yourself or you can gather a group of guys together and pray for one another, asking God to fill each one with the baptism in the Holy Spirit.

It will be a life changing event just like those in Acts whose lives were transformed by coming to know Jesus and by being baptized in the Holy Spirit.

Don't be content living in a home without power!

While none of us could imagine doing so, occasionally when the electricity goes off, we scramble around trying to figure out what to do and how to operate.

I know I need the baptism in the Holy Spirit to empower what I do in my life. Even when doing what I might consider the mundane things of life like working in a church building, the Holy Spirit's guidance is there to encourage, protect, and place me among people who can benefit from what I have to offer.

When asking for the baptism in the Holy Spirit, bear in mind that no one can speak two languages at once. When we sense the overflow of the Spirit inside us and we want to give expression to His work in our hearts, we will have to decide to either speak in the language we know or launch out in faith to say words we may not understand.

The reality, especially with men, is our tendency to overthink what is going on. As I indicated earlier, we have full knowledge of what we are saying, and we are the ones talking. The same holds true to the baptism in the Holy Spirit. We have full knowledge we are saying words, words that we do not have to think about to say. It is a fluent language that to us may seem almost childish, but we know it is authentic because we are communicating to God with a sincere heart.

Having traveled in many countries with a variety of languages, I assure you there is no such thing as word-for-word translation. But because the language has no resemblance to the one I know, is it any less genuine to those who understand the words?

The Bible reminds us in 1 Corinthians 14:10:

> *Undoubtedly there are all sorts of languages in the world, yet none of them is without meaning.* (NIV)

The Holy Spirit will not interrupt us, barge in on us, nor take over our words. It is up to us to give voice, or as many have said, to yield to the Holy Spirit, allowing Him to speak with our mouths with words we do not understand but are willing to say.

The dream is realizing that God wants to do so much more in our lives than we might have thought or could only have dreamed to be possible.

Back to my own story, after a number of years with an internal struggle to follow God's direction in life (a whole other story), I came to the place of surrender to God. I had fully and completely placed my life in the hands and will of God. I promised God to do whatever He wished to do in my life, knowing that would mean getting in front of people to talk.

I was an engineering student at this time, but having made the full surrender to God, I was asked to speak at a church an hour away from my home. I cannot describe the fear I felt when asked, and I agreed to come. I was petrified of failure, of looking foolish, and of letting down God and my family.

I had been filled with the baptism in the Holy Spirit five years earlier, but never fully understood the importance until I was in a place where I knew I was in over my head. I prayed during the whole trip, and many times I wanted to turn around and hide somewhere to get away.

I prayed and prayed while I drove. I had worked to prepare; I had some notes to help me speak, knowing God was not going to do what I could. At that time I was not even sure He would do what I could not do: stand in front of others and be effective.

The power of God was very real that night, and what I can tell you is that once I stood up, I experienced what it meant to be anointed by God to do what I considered the impossible. I was able to communicate effectively and powerfully unlike the leanings of my personality at that time.

I can tell you now, after thirty-three years of communicating the Bible, I still get nervous. But I also still have the touch of God through the baptism in the Holy Spirit which has enabled me to do what I do all these years.

It is not me; it is the power of God through a broken life that touches the lives of others.

BIG IDEA:

The baptism of the Holy Spirit with the evidence of speaking in tongues is God's gift to us. It allows Jesus to more fully work in our lives so that other people may know Jesus. It is our power source for living the Christian life.

GROUP STUDY QUESTIONS:

1. Why is it important to be filled with the baptism of the Holy Spirit?

2. What is the difference between the Holy Spirit's work of conviction and the baptism of the Holy Spirit?

3. Have you been baptized in the Holy Spirit? If yes, tell us when and what it was like?

4. How does speaking in tongues help us pray?

5. The author stated, "Our desire for the baptism in the Holy Spirit is to allow Jesus to more fully work in our lives, that other people may know Jesus." What does this mean?

6. After reading this chapter, what is one thing you will put into practice or one thing you will change in your life?

7. How can we, as a group, help you do this?

26

THE FRUIT OF THE SPIRIT

By: Stan Williams

Don't become so well-adjusted to your culture that you fit into it without even thinking. Instead, fix your attention on God. You'll be changed from the inside out. Readily recognize what he wants from you, and quickly respond to it. Unlike the culture around you, always dragging you down to its level of immaturity, God brings the best out of you, develops well-formed maturity in you. (Romans 12:2, The Message)

This is a challenge for each of us since conforming to our culture seems to happen with little effort. Focusing on God, understanding the need for change, and discovering how change will happen are the first steps to transformation.

Scripture speaks of our walk as a battle that we win as we cooperate with the Holy Spirit within us. The Holy Spirit leads us into the truth, producing fruit in us that is in keeping with the values and truth of God.

WINNING IS A MATTER OF KEEPING IN STEP WITH THE HOLY SPIRIT

But I say, walk by the Spirit, and you will not gratify the desires of the flesh. (Galatians 5:16, NIV)

If we live by the Spirit, let us also keep in step with the Spirit. (Galatians 5:25, ESV)

WHAT IS THE FRUIT THAT THE HOLY SPIRIT PRODUCES IN US?

But the fruit of the Spirit is love, joy, peace, patience, kindness, goodness, faithfulness, gentleness, self-control; against such things there is no law. (Galatians 5:22-23, ESV)

The fruit of the Spirit is supernatural just as the gifts of the Spirit are supernatural. This fruit is produced in our lives by the Holy Spirit with our cooperation.

George O. Wood has said:

"All the characteristics listed in Galatians 5:22, 23— the fruit of the Spirit— are meant to be part of our life. The key to developing fruit is to abide in Christ:

"If a man remains in me and I in him, he will bear much fruit" (John 15: 5).

So let's continue to sink our roots down in Christ. His life will surely grow in us."

LOVE

Without love the gifts of the Spirit will be ineffective!

Natural love loves it own, flourishes in an atmosphere of friendship, and is fed by mutual affection. Only on very rare occasions will natural love persist when no apparent return is given. But the fruit of the Spirit goes beyond all this, for it even produces love for declared enemies.[1]

As a pastor, I encountered difficult and even angry members who seemed to be determined to hinder the forward movement of the ministry. The Holy Spirit made it clear that as their shepherd I needed to love them and feel compassion for them. The fruit of love operating under those conditions proved to be powerful making it possible to love genuinely and to have their best interest at heart.

'You shall love your neighbor and hate your enemy.'

But I say to you, love your enemies, bless those who curse you, do good to those who hate you, and pray for those who spitefully use you and persecute you, that you may be sons of your Father in heaven; for He makes His sun rise on the evil and on the good, and sends rain on the just and on the unjust. For if you love those who love you, what reward have you? (Matthew 5:43-45, NKJV)

JOY

For the kingdom of God is not a matter of eating and drinking but of righteousness and peace and joy in the Holy Spirit. (Romans 14:17, ESV)

We love to be around joyful people and avoid the opportunity to spend time with the angry and complaining ones. I have friends who bring joy into my life. I love to see them coming.

Our joyfulness should not depend on everything going our way. Even in sickness, the joy of the Lord gives us strength. The joy of the follower of Christ is the result of the Holy Spirit within them.

I know the Lord is always with me. I will not be shaken, for he is right beside me.

No wonder my heart is glad, and I rejoice. My body rests in safety. (Psalm 16:8,9, NLT)

Are you someone who brings joy into lives of others?

PEACE

Do not be anxious about anything, but in everything by prayer and supplication with thanksgiving let your requests be made known to God. And the peace of God, which surpasses all understanding, will guard your hearts and your minds in Christ Jesus. (Philippians 4:6-7, ESV)

Today there is much to be anxious about, so our conversations and thoughts focus on the worst possible scenarios. We worry about our families, we worry about the future of America and, yes, the world. As followers, we know that God has the final say, and we should not be surprised at what is happening around us. The ability to leave it with God with thanksgiving brings a guard into our lives and a peace that goes beyond our comprehension. Experiencing peace when there should not be peace is miraculous.

PATIENCE

Better is the end of a thing than the beginning thereof: and the patient in spirit is better than the proud in spirit. Be not hasty in thy spirit to be angry: for anger resteth in the bosom of fools. (Ecclesiastes 7:8-9, KJV)

In recent days, I have been aware that irritability seems to come easier for me. You would think that after seventy years I would have conquered that. It is clear that my irritation is directly connected to a lack of patience. Not wanting to be thought a fool, I am going to respond to the Holy Spirit so that the fruit of patience will become obvious in me.

According to James, patience also develops out of difficult experiences.

Brethren, count it all joy when you fall into various trials, knowing that the testing of your faith produces patience. (James 1:2,-3, NKJV)

I have learned the most about patience from God. Even in my early years of rebellion, He did not leave me or give up on me. The Holy Spirit was the hound of Heaven, just nipping at my heels until I returned wholeheartedly to him.

"True patience is an essentially voluntary thing. God does not have to suffer long with offenders. He does it because *"love is patient, love is kind"* (1 Corinthians 13: 4), and those who show patience do it with a strong purpose of kindness."[2]

How may we keep in step with the Holy Spirit? This brings us to: kindness, goodness and gentleness.

These three are similar so, let's look at them together.

KINDNESS

The fruit of kindness is consideration of others:

> *Be kind to one another, tenderhearted, forgiving one another, as God in Christ forgave you.* (Ephesians 4:32, ESV)

The Lord is a kind Shepherd, always responding with the greatest concern for the sheep in His flock:

> *He will tend his flock like a shepherd; he will gather the lambs in his arms; he will carry them in his bosom, and gently lead those that are with young.* (Isaiah 40:11, NIV)

The average man may have difficulty being tenderhearted, believing that real men are never tenderhearted.

I point to Jesus. No one demonstrated more tenderness than He did. He welcomed the small children, the leper, the lame and the hopeless. He shows us what the qualities of a real man are.

GOODNESS

It means moral excellence, upright. It's not being sanctimonious which comes across as disingenuous. All of us have met individuals who we described as "good, people of character and honest to a fault." These kind of men make great friends. You can trust them to pick you up if you fall and to speak the truth into your life when you need to hear it.

The fruit of goodness draws the non-follower to God:

In the same way, let your light shine before others, so that they may see your good works and give glory to your Father who is in heaven. (Matthew 5:16 ESV)

This brings us to:

GENTLENESS

Gentleness is the ability to control your response to others.

True gentleness is a byproduct of humility, including not taking yourself too seriously and putting others first. These are prerequisites to being used mightily by God. Such men have had an impact on my life.

I often do not succeed in controlling my responses to others, at times coming back with a harsh angry reaction. I have learned, when that happens, the conversation is over and the opportunity to influence is wasted. Such opportunities may not happen again, so learning to respond with wisdom and gentleness may open the door for even greater opportunities to influence someone.

FAITHFULNESS

The fruit of faithfulness is steadfastness, loyalty, an unwillingness to vacillate.

Faithfulness is a necessity in any long-term relationship. I have witnessed the distress caused by unfaithfulness in marriages where entire families have been destroyed.

God, Himself, is the greatest example for us. His faithfulness has never failed. Even when we drop the ball, He is faithful.

God is faithful, through whom ye were called into the fellowship of his Son Jesus Christ our Lord. (1 Corinthians 1:9, ASV)

When we participate with the Holy Spirit, the fruit of faithfulness is developed within us, becoming the life of any Spirit-led follower of Jesus Christ.

Joshua left a parting message to Israel, telling them to choose, and setting the example of steadfast, faithfulness to God.

> *If it is evil in your eyes to serve the Lord, choose this day whom you will serve, whether the gods your fathers served in the region beyond the River, or the gods of the Amorites in whose land you dwell. But as for me and my house, we will serve the Lord.* (Joshua 24:15, ESV)

Finally, the last fruit of the Spirit is:

SELF-CONTROL

When we exercise self-control in every area of our lives, it is a sign of spiritual growth.

A great example of self-control is that of Joseph in Potiphar's house. Not only did he resist the advances of his master's wife for days, but actually fled when there was no other way of escape.

An important response of self-control may often be running or getting out of the place of temptation. I urge you to read again this powerful true story of Joseph in Genesis chapter 39.

Joseph's final answer to Potiphar's wife is an example for each of us to live by.

> *How then can I do this great wickedness and sin against God?"* (Genesis 39:9b, ESV)

Our desire for the fruit of the Spirit in our lives is primarily motivated by our love for God and our desire to bring glory to Him.

HOW DO WE KEEP IN STEP WITH THE HOLY SPIRIT?

Obviously, to keep in step with another you must know them, communicate with them, and love being with them. Communication is important to any healthy relationship. It is here that we often fail, finding it easy to zone out and not even relate to the one across the table. I have been accused of this behavior, causing those closest to me to believe I just am not interested in what they have to say.

The Holy Spirit does not suddenly pack up and leave when we seem unattached. We may not be aware of his presence, but He is with us always. So how may we keep in step with the Spirit?

ACKNOWLEDGE HIS PRESENCE

My dad used to say, "If we walked with earthly friends the way we walk with God, they wouldn't walk with us for very long."

Imagine spending a day with a friend who never spoke a word to you. Trust me, future opportunities would not be looked forward to. Yet, we may go through minutes, hours, and yes, even days, without uttering a word to the Holy Spirit.

> *Know ye not that your body is a temple of the Holy Spirit which is in you, which ye have from God?* (1 Corinthians 6:19, ASV)

So we must acknowledge His presence and we must:

PAY ATTENTION TO THE TEACHER

> *When the Spirit of truth comes, he will guide you into all the truth,* (John 16:13, ESV)

As the Spirit guides you, He is helping you to understand truth. His tutelage makes Bible study an adventure that leads to a destination. Any class is exciting when the teacher is interested in you and what He shares is life-changing.

This may be a good opportunity to turn to John chapters 14 & 16 to further understand the value of the Spirit's work inside of you.

WHAT COULD BE MORE VALUABLE TO A FOLLOWER THAN UNDERSTANDING GOD'S TRUTH?

The changes the Holy Spirit is affecting in me will happen when I commit daily to cooperate with Him. This commitment is not driven by insecurity or fear, but a love for God and a desire to be more like

Christ. More than ever, I want to keep in step with the Spirit!

> *If we live by the Spirit, let us also keep in step with the Spirit.* (Galatians 5:25, ESV)

LIVE THE WISDOM

When we understand God's truth we must then do it!

Knowing has little value when it does not include doing. Truth must always impact values and actions, setting us free by transforming how we think and react.

Don't fool yourself into thinking that you are a listener when you are anything but, letting the Word go in one ear and out the other. Act on what you hear! Those who hear and don't act are like those who glance in the mirror, walk away, and two minutes later have no idea who they are, what they look like.

> *But whoever catches a glimpse of the revealed counsel of God— the free life!—even out of the corner of his eye, and sticks with it, is no distracted scatterbrain but a man or woman of action. That person will find delight and affirmation in the action.* (James 1:22-25, The Message)

When you live the truth that the Holy Spirit has made clear to those around, you are affected. Your influence becomes powerful and life changing, turning the light on for others and revealing the goodness of God.

When the Fruit of the Spirit rather than the works of the flesh mark your life, people want to know why. Your changed life is a powerful testimony of the power of the Gospel. So, keep in step!

BIG IDEA:

When the Fruit of the Spirit rather than the works of the flesh mark your life, people want to know why. Your changed life is a powerful testimony of the power of the Gospel.

GROUP STUDY QUESTIONS:

1. How are the works of the flesh hindering you in your relationship with God and others?

2. Discuss how keeping in step with the Holy Spirit is obvious in your own life. What steps are you presently taking, and how can you improve in this area?

3. The Fruit of the Spirit is directly related to the brightness of your light and the saltiness of your influence. How would a greater cooperation with the Holy Spirit enlarge your influence with non-believers you are in contact with?

4. After reading this chapter, what is one thing you will put into practice or one thing you will change in your life?

5. How can we, as a group, help you do this?

27

HANDLING PERSECUTION THROUGH THE POWER OF THE HOLY SPIRIT

By: Tom Sember

Starting a new construction project can bring about a mess of red tape as you try to get permits, variances, and other things needed to complete the project on time. There will also be things that are out of your control like delivery schedules, trucks breaking down, and even the occasional bad weather. All these together can create an atmosphere where a builder can get discouraged and want to throw in the towel, saying that the project just isn't worth it all!

In life, living according to God's Word can also bring moments where our walk with Christ will be difficult. We will face many problems, difficulties, and struggles along the way. Sometimes the struggles, persecution, and/or oppression can come through the church itself. It's times like these that we should recognize what we have available to us, a certain power to overcome.

When Jesus was physically on this earth, He was beginning His new church. He walked with the disciples and taught them by His actions and His parables. After the work on the cross and His resurrection, He knew His time on this earth was coming to a close, so He gathered His followers and spoke these important words to them. It is recorded for us:

> *But you will receive power when the Holy Spirit has come upon you; and you shall be My witnesses both in Jerusalem, and in all Judea and Samaria, and even to the remotest part of the earth.* (Acts 1:8, NASB)

When the foreman on the job site wants to share some important information, he gathers the head of each department for a meeting. He begins to lay out plans on how and why certain things need to be done in order for the project to move forward. This is pretty much what Jesus did with His followers. The foreman will give out specific instructions on how best to accomplish the tasks that will need to be done in order to finish the job well.

Jesus shared the most important information we need, to finish the job of being godly men in an ungodly world, *"you will receive power when the Holy Spirit has come upon you..."*

When I was building houses, I had days when it seemed like everything was against me, little things that caused me to step back and ask why.

"Why was the delivery date of the material going to be late?"

"Why did my hammer have to break when I needed it the most?"

"Why did the other men call in sick making it impossible to finish the list of things needed to be done?"

It was during these moments, when I realized that some things are out of my control, and the best I can do is face them one at a time.

When we, men, begin to live for Christ, we will face some things that may seem like the world is against us. People will be questioning whether or not it's real. Some guys we work with will begin to see changes in our lifestyle and begin to challenge us as to why we aren't the same guy. People outside of work will begin to call us things like "Jesus freaks," "holy rollers," and even worst "Christians." It is during these times when we need the power that Christ spoke of during His final moments on this earth.

So how do we go about handling persecution and oppression as godly men?

It may seem like such a simple answer, and yet it will require us to let go of what we think we know and who we think we are, and rely on the power of the Holy Spirit.

Let me give you an example from my life:

I grew up with an anger problem. Little things would set me off into a tyrant of abusive language and even physical outbursts like throwing coffee cups, punching walls, etc. It was not a pretty sight.

When I came to know Jesus as Lord and Savior, I thought the anger would cease, but sadly it did not. It wasn't like I didn't pray to have it taken away, but, in my own power, I was helpless to make it happen.

Only once baptized in the Holy Spirit, did I begin to see that it was the power I needed to stand firm against the tricks of satan. On my own I couldn't change, but change came when I was walking in the power of the Holy Spirit. The things that set me off were still there, but with the Holy Spirit, I found the power to walk towards a place that became more about Him and not me.

Jesus went on to say in that verse (Acts 1:8) that we would be His witnesses.

As I thought about that statement, "His witnesses," I thought of how the houses that I built, the jobs that I had done, are a witness to my integrity as a builder and craftsman. If I did a shoddy job, people would see me as a shoddy craftsman. If I did the best that I could do, the witness of my work would be entirely different.

Our walk with Christ is the greatest witness of His Power to those we share life with, so making it a good one, filled with integrity, honesty, and purity, can be found through the power of the Holy

Spirit.

Let's get specific about handling persecution and oppression in our life and some things we can do to walk in the power of the Holy Spirit.

Paul wrote some great advice to the Romans.

Rejoicing in hope, persevering in tribulation, devoted to prayer, (Romans 12:12, NASB)

REJOICE IN HOPE

We can always find things that we can rejoice in.

Even when the job site may be filled with difficulties, we can rejoice in the hope that He is in control, that things will get better. In our walk as Christian men, we may find that the road we are on is a difficult path, people questioning our faith, our actions, our decisions, but if we rejoice in the hope of Christ, we will find the strength to carry on.

PERSEVERE IN TRIBULATIONS

"Persevere in tribulations" means getting through the pain of the difficulties.

We were finishing putting the roof shingles on a new house we had built, when the weather had turned cold and snow began to fall. Our fingers were freezing, the snow made the roof difficult to walk on, and yet we carried on. Why? Because the job had to be done in order to finish what we started.

When our life becomes difficult, people questioning our faith and walk with Christ, we must persevere in the power of the Holy Spirit.

Why? Because Jesus went all the way to the cross for you and me. He didn't find excuses to quit; He carried on in the power of the Spirit. So can we.

DEVOTED TO PRAYER

Prayer keeps our mind on things above, so when the persecution comes, and it will come, we will be prayed-up to face the battle. Praying in the Spirit, groaning in words that we don't understand, can give our spirit the peace that only Christ can bring.

Facing persecution and oppression in our walk with Christ will take us to the point where we need to stand up and be the men we are called to be. By ourselves we may be powerless, but in the power of the Holy Spirit, all things are possible.

The story of Nehemiah is a great example to us of a builder who set out to rebuild the walls of the temple in Jerusalem. He ran into persecution when some men began to question why he was doing what he was doing. They even began to ridicule their work saying, "What are these feeble Jews doing?"

One man even stated:

> *Even what they are building-if a fox should jump on it, he would break their stone wall down.* (Neh.4:3, NASB)

Nehemiah turned to God to find the strength for himself and the other builders. They put their faith in God and the power of His Spirit to continue the work they were called to do.

He even went so far as to say to the men doing the work:

> *Do not be afraid of them; remember the Lord who is great and awesome, and fight for your brothers, your sons, your daughters, your wives and your houses.* (Nehemiah 4:14, NASB)

As men, we are called to be builders of God's Kingdom here on earth. We are to be builders of our families, our churches, and our communities by building relationships with other men to stand firm against the world. No power on earth can stand against the power of God and the power of the Holy Spirit.

When we face persecution and oppression, we can find the power to stand firm in the power of the Holy Spirit. Now there are certain things we can be doing to help stand firm:

1. SEEK THE BAPTISM IN THE HOLY SPIRIT

We may have heard the gospel of Jesus Christ and accepted Him as our Lord and Savior, but it doesn't end there. That would be like building just the foundation of a house and not going any further and calling it a home. We need to begin to build the walls, roof, windows, and doors to complete the house project. In the same way, we must begin to build upon the foundation of Christ. Seeking the baptism of the Holy Spirit is our next course of action.

2. PRAY

When building a house, we need to make sure we are in communication with the architect so that the house is built to proper specs. Prayer keeps us in communication with God, the ultimate Architect of life.

3. READ HIS WORD

When building, we need to go back to the blueprints to make sure the measurements are in line and accurate. God's Word is our blueprint for learning and staying true and plumb in our walk with Christ.

4. GATHERING WITH OTHER MEN

Any workman knows that a good crew can make the difference in any project. A good crew of godly men, to help us stay on task, is essential for living the Christian life.

5. WALK IN THE SPIRIT

Using a tool that is not working to it's full potential can lead to trouble. Walking the Christian life without the power of the Holy Spirit will lead to trouble. Our tools need to be charged to full power; so should our walk be charged to full power of the Holy Spirit.

BIG IDEA:

When we face persecution and oppression, we can find the courage to stand firm in the power of the Holy Spirit. This power will give us the strength to persevere and overcome!

GROUP STUDY QUESTIONS:

1. Building on our foundation of Jesus Christ, what does it mean to be baptized by the Holy Spirit? (Read Acts 2.)

2. Have you been baptized in the Holy Spirit for the building up of the body of Christ?

3. What persecution or oppression have you faced while building your life with Christ?

4. What are some tools you can use when handling persecution or oppression as we build for Christ?

5. Are you a member of a crew (a group of Christian brothers) that you can turn to when the persecution becomes too hard to handle alone?

6. How does Paul's story of the thorn in his side, relate to handling persecution or oppression in your life? (Read 2 Corinthians 12:7-9)

7. After reading this chapter, what is one thing you will put into practice or one thing you will change in your life?

8. How can we, as a group, help you do this?

SECTION 6:

Moving In: Reaching Your Full Potential As A Man Of God

-28-

BECOMING PART OF A CHURCH COMMUNITY

by Jason Tourville

I have always loved being a part of a team. From my earliest memories at the YMCA playing in a recreational basketball league, to backyard tackle football, sports teams are where I found my belonging and identity. In some ways, it is also where I found my worth.

As a family, we moved ten times during my childhood. Every couple of years I found myself in a new school, in a new house, setting up my new room. Of course, this also forced me to constantly make new friends. For me, this typically happened around sports. From the backyard to the blacktop, new friendships were formed.

Because of a neck injury, I had to abandon my calling as the next high-profile wide-receiver at the age of nine. My attention turned to basketball. The competition, the struggle, and the battles that were waged on the basketball court formed a type of bond. Those on my team would become more than friends, we were teammates. They were my brothers.

Through the years I would play on dozens of teams and with multiple teammates. High school and college teams formed the deepest relational ties. To this day, I know that I could call those on my college team at any moment, and they would be there for me. Brothers!

This is the type of belonging and connection I began to miss in my early adult years. At twenty-one years old I got married, graduated Bible College, and soon found myself in a new community, working as a youth pastor. My closest friends were finishing out their senior year, so our lives, as well as our relationships, changed drastically.

Loneliness and isolation were never something I had faced before. I'm not whining, but this 1-2 combination hit me hard, and I never saw it coming. It is not that I didn't have relationships. As a pastor and leader, I was surrounded by people constantly. My relationship with my new bride was great, and I loved being married. I just didn't have my brothers anymore. That sense of belonging and brotherhood was lost.

FINDING A NEW TEAM

When I read about the First Century church (those that believed and followed Jesus and His "way" after He went back up to heaven), I get a sense that they experienced in their spiritual gatherings what I had experienced on my sports team. In fact, they had a name for it! In their language they called it *koinonia*.

Like many translated words, it is difficult to find one English word to describe its meaning. To summarize, *koinonia* means to have a real relationship, in which life and struggles and victories are all shared. It is to belong to something bigger than yourself. In essence it blends together the best of relationships and purpose together. It is to have "something in common." *Koinonia* is the Jesus Team!

Perhaps like me, you have felt the lack of this *koinonia* in your life as an adult man. Maybe you have your wife, kids, co-workers, etc... but you miss being a part of that "team." Well, I have good news for you, God knows that as a man you have a need for this type of belonging and has provided the context for these relationships. It's called the CHURCH!

BECOMING PART OF GOD'S TEAM

Confession: I'm a church brat. My parents raised me in church. I cut my teeth on the corner of the hymn books, and learned to crawl escaping my mother underneath the pews. Because of my background, I love the church. As imperfect as she is at times, I'm a fan. Even if you've been hurt by or taken offense to someone in the church, I still want to encourage you to become a part of God's team, the church.

As a "fan" of the church, I am always taken back at how quickly many men "jump-ship" when it comes to their relationship with the church. It's not that I don't sympathize when someone is hurt, an ill-word is spoken, a misunderstanding is never corrected, or an imperfect leader (which we all are) makes a mistake. Still, as men, we are not hardwired to be fair-weathered fans.

Maybe this is because I'm an Eagles fan. Most of us have a love/hate relationship with our team. We are committed for life, but at times it feels like a life-sentence. Even when the Eagles begin with a winning record, there is something in us as fans that knows not to rejoice too quickly. At the end of every painful season, the faith-filled phrase falls from our lips, "There's always next year."

When the movie "Invincible" came out in the theatres, Mark Wahlberg's portrayal of a Philadelphia Eagles fan was classic. What really captured the imagination of every man was that Mark's character, Vince Papale, moved out of the stand and onto the playing field. He was no longer just a fan, now he was part of the team.

As a man of God, I want to briefly give you some practical steps to becoming a real part of God's team. It's time for men to move out of the bleachers and onto the field.

To become an active teammate on God's team, it takes one quality: COMMITMENT. Nothing is ever accomplished without commitment. The following 4 Commitments will radically change your experience and will radically change you in the process:

4 COMMITMENTS FOR GOD'S TEAM:

1. I WILL PROTECT THE UNITY OF MY CHURCH

No team or church has ever accomplished anything of substance without unity. This doesn't mean that everyone is the same or even has the same perspective all the time. You can have unity without uniformity. Be yourself, but be unified. Here's how:

... BY ACTING IN LOVE TOWARD OTHER MEMBERS AND REFUSING TO GOSSIP

Now that you have purified yourselves by obeying the truth so that you have sincere love for each other, love one another deeply, from the heart. (1 Peter 1:22, NIV)

... BY HOLDING TO THE TEACHINGS OF THE CHURCH

Do not let any unwholesome talk come out of your mouths, but only what is helpful for building others up according to their needs, that it may benefit those who listen. (Ephesians 4:29, NIV)

... BY DEVELOPING A SERVANT'S HEART

You, my brothers and sisters, were called to be free. But do not use your freedom to indulge the flesh; rather, serve one another humbly in love. (Galatians 5:13, NIV)

2. I WILL SHARE THE RESPONSIBILITIES OF MY CHURCH

Can you imagine a football player who is drafted to a team who doesn't want to practice, show up at team meetings, sit in the team locker room, watch the film, or even "suit-up" in their uniform for game-time? That would be ridiculous. Unfortunately, there are many people who approach God's team in this manner. Here are three ways to share in the responsibilities of God's team:

... BY PRAYING FOR ITS EFFECTIVENESS IN MINISTRY AND OUTREACH

Pray also for me, that whenever I speak, words may be given me so that I will fearlessly make known the mystery of the gospel, (Ephesians 6:19, NIV)

... BY FINANCIALLY GIVING REGULARLY

On the first day of every week, each one of you should set aside a sum of money in keeping with your income, (1 Corinthians 16:2a, NIV)

A tenth of all you receive is the Lord's and is holy.

... BY WARMLY WELCOMING THOSE WHO VISIT

Accept (welcome) one another, then, just as Christ accepted you, in order to bring praise to God. (Romans 15:7, NIV)

3. I WILL SERVE THE MISSION OF MY CHURCH

A coach's job is to get EVERYONE on the team moving in the same direction, working towards the same goal, and looking out for one another. This is also critically important in a church.

Towards this purpose, God gives spiritual leaders in the church. These men and women of God are just like you (made of flesh), but with a different role. They have responded to God's call to lead his team. They are most productive and effective when those in the church respond to them in the following ways:

... BY DISCOVERING MY GIFTS AND TALENTS

Each of you should use whatever gift you have received to serve others, as faithful stewards of God's grace in its various forms. (1 Peter 4:10, NIV)

... BY BEING EQUIPPED BY MY PASTORS TO SERVE

So Christ himself gave... {spiritual leaders}, to equip his people for works of service, so that the body of Christ may be built up. (Ephesians 4:11-12, NIV)

... BY FOLLOWING THE LEADERSHIP

> *Have confidence in your leaders and submit to their authority, because they keep watch over you as those who must give an account. Do this so that their work will be a joy, not a burden, for that would be of no benefit to you.* (Hebrews 13:17, NIV)

4. I WILL SUPPORT THE TESTIMONY OF MY CHURCH

You not only represent Jesus with your life, but you represent His Church. Bringing Christ's life and love to our world depends a great deal on our testimony and reputation. Jesus said it this way:

> *All people will know that you are my followers if you love each other.* (John 13:35, NCV)

We support this testimony in the following actions:

... BY ATTENDING FAITHFULLY

> *Not giving up meeting together, as some are in the habit of doing, but encouraging one another—and all the more as you see the Day approaching.* (Hebrews 10:25, NIV)

...BY LIVING A GODLY LIFE

> *Whatever happens, conduct yourselves in a manner worthy of the gospel of Christ. Then, whether I come and see you or only hear about you in my absence, I will know that you stand firm in the one Spirit, striving together as one for the faith of the gospel.* (Philippians 1:27, NIV)

...BY INVITING THE UNCHURCHED TO ATTEND

> *Then the master told his servant, 'Go out to the roads and country lanes and compel them to come in, so that my house will be full.'* (Luke 14:23, NIV)

God has recruited you to His team. Together with your teammates, His church, you can build something great together. As the construction of your life, as well as the construction on God's Kingdom (His team) takes place, moving in and becoming a part of a church community, makes it possible.

We are BETTER TOGETHER! Let's build something great.

BIG IDEA:

We are called to help build up the body of Christ. This is done by us becoming an active part of our church. We need to become a part of our church body, supporting it both financially and with our time. Our church is only as strong and as effective as its members. We are better together!

GROUP STUDY QUESTIONS:

1. How does being active in your church meet a need inside of you?

2. Why is unity key to being part of your church?

3. What can you do to share responsibility in your church?

4. What is your church's mission? How can you support it?

5. After reading this chapter, what is one thing you will put into practice or one thing you will change in your life?

6. How can we, as a group, help you do this?

GOING OUTSIDE OF THE CHURCH COMMUNITY

By: Terry Drost

British minister, Charles Spurgeon once challenged his hearers with these convicting words: *"Have you no wish for others to be saved? Then you are not saved yourself. Be sure of that."*[1]

Spurgeon's words ring relevant for today and should quickly prompt us to evaluate whether or not we are effectively reaching out to our local community, beyond the walls of the church, with a genuine desire to see the lives of others deeply changed by the Gospel.

In these next brief moments, we are going to explore the Biblical importance of sharing the Gospel within our community, what prevents us from sharing our faith outside our church community, and what it looks like to live out the Gospel in our community.

DOES THE BIBLE REALLY SAY THAT WE'RE CALLED TO SHARE THE GOSPEL IN OUR COMMUNITIES?

I've heard several Christians question whether or not living out the Gospel in their local context is found in Scripture. These are a few key passages that help us answer this question.

In Genesis 12:1-3, God begins unveiling His redemptive plan to Abraham:

> *The Lord had said to Abram, "Go from your country, your people and your father's household to the land I will show you. I will make you into a great nation, and I will bless you; I will make your name great, and you will be a blessing. I will bless those who bless you, and whoever curses you I will curse; and all peoples on earth will be blessed through you."* (NIV)

In this passage, God is not saying that He is merely choosing to bless a nation with resources so that they can hoard everything for themselves and live happily ever after. Rather, God is revealing to Abraham His purpose for Israel, and for us: to be His mouthpiece, to other nations, along with the people surrounding our community, to place their faith in God.

The Bible not only tells us to go into our community, but commands it:

> *All authority in heaven and on earth has been given to me. Therefore go and make disciples of all nations, baptizing them in the name of the Father and of the Son and of the Holy Spirit, and teaching them to obey everything I have commanded you. And surely I am with you always, to the very end of the age.* (Matthew 28:18-20, NIV)

When examining the Greek grammar in verses 19-20, "*make disciples*" (mathēteuō) is an imperative, or a command,[2] which means "*to train as a disciple; to teach, to instruct.*"[3]

In other words, Jesus' final words before He ascends to heaven are commanding His eleven disciples to make even more disciples. Jesus uses the Greek word, *ta ethnē*, for "*all nations*" in the Greek which means "*people groups.*"[4] This passage is God's message to us to make committed disciples for Christ as opposed to fleeting first-time decisions to follow Him.

WHAT PREVENTS US FROM SHARING OUR FAITH OUTSIDE OUR CHURCH COMMUNITY?

Have you ever seen a great building or a wonder of the world such as the Empire State Building, the White House, the Taj Mahal, or the Great Pyramid of Giza? Instead of marveling at the whole structure itself, what if you chose to direct your fascination towards the smallest detail? One of the windows in the Empire State Building, or a casing stone firmly packed into the pyramid, or one of the hedges outside of the White House garden, or one of the minarets placed alongside the Taj Mahal.

I can speak for myself when I say that I have never done that!

Although I haven't seen all the places I mentioned in person, the places I have been to cause me to marvel at the whole structure or in other words, "the big picture" of what each architect and builder were trying to convey.

So you may be wondering, what does this have to do with anything?

I mention this because, when it comes to living out God's purpose in our everyday lives, our focus can easily become zoomed in on all the details and prevent us from seeing the "big picture" of how God is trying to use us in the everyday rhythms of life. This is especially true when it comes to living out our faith outside the four walls of the church building and going into our communities equipped to share the Gospel message with others to make more disciples for Christ.

The "details" or "distractions" that we can become easily consumed with can be work, money, marriage, health, sports, relationships, knowledge, our possessions, and so on. Although each of these things are gifts from God, if we are not careful, it is easy for each of these details to point us away from Christ and His mission instead of pointing us toward Him.

Jesus describes these types of people in His parable of the sower:

The seed that fell among thorns stands for those who hear, (the Gospel) but as they go on their way they are choked by life's worries, riches and pleasures, and they do not mature. (Luke 8:14, NIV)

In this text, Jesus is challenging His hearers not to be so quick to assume that they are the "good seed."

It is easy to think that we are the "good seed" when we attend church every Sunday, give our tithe, and join a small group. The difference between the good seed and the seed that fell among the thorns is that the good seed would, *"hear the word and accept it and bear fruit, thirtyfold and sixtyfold and a hundredfold."* (Mark 4:20, NIV)

In other words, what makes the good seed different from the seed among the thorns consists of the good seed bearing and multiplying fruit. They understand God's Word and put it into practice both inside and outside of our church community.

WHAT DOES SHARING OUR FAITH OUTSIDE OUR COMMUNITY LOOK LIKE?

As a Christian, we are called to serve our outside community alongside our local church and be the church in the everyday rhythms of life.

IN OUR CHURCH COMMUNITY

When it comes to serving the outside community through your local church, there are numerous ways to serve. This is awesome, because the body of Christ consists of people who have diverse giftings and resources.

For those of you who have been blessed with the resource of finances, maybe serving your community through your local church means funding a community outreach such as a food drive or clothing drive. Or maybe it means contributing to a building program for your local church that will help reach out to your community.

Maybe some of you who enjoy sports and are athletic could contribute to your local community by heading up a sports camp through your church or a sports league such as softball, golf, Frisbee, basketball, or any other sports.

There are so many different ways to serve your community through your local church. All you have to do is see where your giftings lie, and go from there!

IN OUR EVERYDAY LIVES

Doing life with others outside our church community in a God-pleasing way means that we must reach out to our community without selling out. Jesus discusses this characteristic to teach His followers at the time, and us, what a genuine follower of Christ looks like in His Sermon on the Mount:

> You are the salt of the earth. But if the salt loses its saltiness, how can it be made salty again? It is no longer good for anything, except to be thrown out and trampled underfoot.
>
> You are the light of the world. A town built on a hill cannot be hidden. Neither do people light a lamp and put it under a bowl. Instead they put it on its stand, and it gives light to everyone in the house. In the same way, let your light shine before others, that they may see your good deeds and glorify your Father in heaven. (Matthew 5:13-16, NIV)

All of us are surrounded with non-Christians such as family members, our neighbors, our co-workers, those who wait on us at the grocery store or at restaurants, along with others we encounter on a daily basis. When we walk through life wearing a more Gospel-focused lens, we become more intentional with our interactions among others.

This causes us to become strategic with how we can build relationships with those surrounding us which can lead them to believing in and being changed by the Gospel.

As Christians, it's easy for us to place sole responsibility on the pastor to deliver a powerful Sunday sermon that will change the life of a first-time guest. We minimize our responsibility as a Christian to consistently build and cultivate bonds with non-Christians who we encounter on a day-to-day basis.

If you are surrounded with non-Christian co-workers, neighbors, etc., discover what common ground you have with each other such as sports, music, movies, food, books, working out, and use that as an opportunity to get to know each other and build a friendship.

If you have a group of buddies who enjoy playing golf, pick a day out of the week, or as your schedule permits, to golf together and get to know their story. As you bond with these individuals, the Holy Spirit will give you timely words to speak to that person, along with an opportunity for you to invite them to a Sunday service or small group. Maybe you could even share your own story of how the Gospel has changed your life.

Before we part ways, I will once again leave you with Spurgeon's challenging words, *"Have you no wish for others to be saved? Then you are not saved yourself. Be sure of that."*

May these words continually compel us to serve our local community by going out and sharing the Good News of the Gospel with those surrounding us.

BIG IDEA:

God didn't just call pastors to reach out to the community. He called us all to leave the safety of our church walls and to reach out to others. Our job is to find creative ways to reach them, while also reaching those in our sphere of influence.

GROUP STUDY QUESTIONS:

1. Who is called to reach out to their communities?

2. What is a way you could personally work to reach your community?

3. What can your men's group do to reach your community?

4. Who are people around you that you could reach out to in your life?

5. After reading this chapter, what is one thing you will put into practice or one thing you will change in your life?

6. How can we, as a group, help you do this?

-30-

CONVERSATIONS THAT SHARE
YOUR FAITH

By: Lee Rogers

Not long ago I was a passenger on a long distance train from Baltimore to Southern Florida, traveling to an academic conference to present a paper. I had just wrapped up a particularly busy season of life, and I took the train because I was looking forward to the lengthy travel time removed from the busyness of everyday life. I hoped to focus on catching up on classwork and preparing for the presentation.

In the evening, I headed to the dining car for dinner, taking a book along with me. I had never eaten in a dining car so I wasn't exactly sure what to expect, but I had a vision of what it might look like. I pictured myself sitting at a private table, leisurely reading my book while enjoying a meal and occasionally gazing out the window at the passing scenery. What actually occurred was far different.

A hostess met me at the entrance of the dining car and led me to a table where a man and a woman were already seated. It appeared my idealized private dinner would not become a reality.

Instead, I would dine across a table from two strangers. They did not seem to know each other, and had also been randomly sat together. They were both staring at their phones in an effort to avoid making eye contact or having an awkward conversation with someone they didn't know. As I sat down I was tempted to do the same, but then I sensed God wanted to use the situation to build an opportunity to share my faith.

BUILDING OPPORTUNITIES TO SHARE THE GOSPEL

One of our primary functions as followers of Christ is to share our faith with those around us. (Matthew 28:19-20, Acts 1:8) This is what Jesus did and what He trained His disciples to do in His absence. It's impossible to call ourselves true followers of Christ unless we are doing the same. The apostle Paul recognized this solemn duty when he proclaimed:

> *We are therefore Christ's ambassadors, as though God were making his appeal through us.* (2 Corinthians 5:20, NIV)

Although we recognize evangelism is a primary duty, most of us are scared to death to share our faith with others, especially with complete strangers. There's a saying, *"Christians and non-Christians have one thing in common: they both hate evangelism."*[1]

If you've ever felt scared to share your faith with another, be assured you're not alone. That's how I was feeling that day in the train car. However, I also felt a sense of relief because I knew that it wasn't my job to save anyone from their sins; that's Jesus' job. My role is only to point them to the cross. That is what I sensed God wanted me to do in that moment.

The best I could do over a meal was build a moment of opportunity to transmit my faith in a genuine and authentic way that would be well-received and perhaps even accepted. Building that kind of opportunity requires more than just communicating the raw facts of the Gospel—any book or website could do that. Building an opportunity means building a conversation, an exchange to get to know one another better in mutual respect so that when my faith is shared, it doesn't fall on insensitive ears.

Building a conversation is the best hope for sharing the gospel with another person. According to the Institute for American Church Growth, 75-90% of new Christians make a commitment to Jesus through a friend who explains the Gospel on an individual, conversational basis.[2] The good news is, it's easy to build a conversation that can connect to Jesus; there are just a few things you'll need in order to build a conversation effectively.

THE FOUNDATION OF THE HOLY SPIRIT

Every good building has a good foundation, and building a conversation is no different. That foundation is the understanding that the Holy Spirit is at work drawing the lost to Jesus, and that same Spirit wants to work through you to share the message of the Gospel. (John 15:26, John 16:8, Luke 12:12, Acts 1:8)

That means every person we meet who needs to hear about Jesus is already being spoken to by the Holy Spirit (whether they know it or not), and that the Spirit will likely want to continue speaking through us.

But how can we know if the Holy Spirit wants to use us at any particular moment? The answer is simple—prayer.

As I sat in that dining car across from two complete strangers, I silently prayed, "God, if this is a moment that you want to speak through me, I am willing. Help me recognize how the Holy Spirit is working."

Prayer that recognizes and harnesses the Holy Spirit's work is foundational and must always be present if we are to build a conversation that leads to Jesus. This type of prayer sensitizes us to the Spirit's guidance and focuses our thoughts on God's agenda. When my prayer was concluded, I opened my mouth and began to speak.

A TOOL BOX FULL OF OTHERS-CENTERED QUESTIONS

"What are your names?" I asked.

Looking up from his phone, somewhat startled, the man replied, "Raheem."

"I'm Carolyn," the woman shyly responded.

I introduced myself and continued to ask them questions about themselves. I listened, learned, and responded with more questions. Carolyn was returning home after visiting her sister. She was in retirement, but it wasn't going well. Her husband had abandoned her ten years prior. She was suddenly alone, struggling to pay off a house and take care of bills that were once shared. The heaviness of life's unfulfilled expectations was evident in her face and in her story.

Raheem had spent his entire life in New York City, where he worked as a bouncer at various nightclubs. At fifty-years old, this was only his eighth time outside New York City. He was traveling to seek out the possibility of a new life in North Carolina. He had recently been diagnosed with MS, and his girlfriend of seven-years had been diagnosed with stage-three cancer. Always a self-empowered man, he had come to the end of his natural power and was searching for more.

We sat in that dining car and talked for over two hours—we were the last to leave, by a long shot. How was it possible for three people of different generations and completely different backgrounds to have such a long conversation?

It was because I was equipped with a toolbox full of questions. Conversations are formed largely by the questions that are asked, so if you want to have a great conversation, you must start by asking great questions.[3]

Great conversations are also others-centered, which means you've got to ask people questions about themselves. I only needed to ask Raheem and Carolyn a few questions about themselves to get them talking, and soon they shared some of the most painful and personal details of their lives with me. The amazing thing was that I only uttered a few words. They did most of the talking.

A BLUEPRINT TO FOLLOW

It may seem crazy or misguided to ask questions about the other person when your ultimate goal is to share Jesus, but there is a blueprint at work; a plan to connect the conversation to Jesus, and that plan centers on you.

Most people will eventually realize they are talking on and on about themselves and will begin to ask you about yourself. Some will do it just to be polite, but most will have a sincere interest in you because you took the time to hear their story first. When it comes time to share your story, if God is truly meaningful in your life, you should be sharing how faith in Christ has impacted your life in one way or another.

Carolyn was the first to ask me a question about myself. I can't talk about my life, my passions, or how I spend my time without talking about Christ and the church, so it didn't take long for the conversation to move into spiritual matters. Since we were already talking about my belief, I felt comfortable asking both of them about their beliefs.

Carolyn was a devoted Catholic, but in sadness she said, "God doesn't see me now. It's like I'm hidden behind a pole." Then she added, "But I still pray every day."

My next question for her was simple: "If you don't believe God sees you, what drives you to pray every day?"

Raheem had never been to church, and instead believed that the power to be God rested within himself. But now life's circumstances were leading him to question that belief. He had begun to read the Bible a little bit, and was looking into Buddhism.

When he found out I was a minister, Raheem immediately called his girlfriend. He was amazed at the coincidence of meeting a minister at a time in life when he was asking so many questions, and he just had to tell her about it. He had simple searching questions for me, "What is it like to be married? I've never thought about that before the last few months," and "How many times has the Bible been changed?" We had a great spiritual conversation.

AN ONGOING PROJECT

At the end of our time in the dining car, I prayed with Raheem and Carolyn. They requested my information so we could keep in contact, and I gladly gave it to them. Neither of them accepted Christ on that occasion, but I was okay with that because I know that coming to faith in Jesus is an ongoing project. It is rarely completed after one great conversation.

On the contrary, the average person must hear the Gospel 7.6 times before they develop faith to believe in Jesus.[4] The Apostle Paul told the Corinthians that one person plants the seed, another waters the seed, but it is God who causes the growth. (1 Corinthians 3:6-7)

When the time is right in the conversation, be prepared to invite someone to accept faith in Jesus. The Holy Spirit may guide you in that direction, but also be prepared with the knowledge that someone else may water the seed you've planted, and another may harvest it.

If you want to learn more about building conversations that connect to Jesus, check out my book Initiate: Powerful Conversations that Lead to Jesus.[5]

BIG THOUGHT:

Most people come to faith in Jesus Christ through a friend who explains the Gospel through a conversation. So if we want to share Jesus effectively, we've got to learn how to have great conversations that connect to Jesus.

GROUP STUDY QUESTIONS:

1. Think about a great conversation you had at some point in life. What made that conversation great? What can you learn from that to have more great conversations?

2. When was the last time you prayed that God would help you share your faith with another person? What opportunities will you have to build a conversation that can connect to faith in the next thirty days? What will you do to prepare yourself?

3. What questions could you ask someone to get them to talk about themselves? Make a list so you can remember them for later use.

4. What significant personal experience with God, testimony, or story of faith can you share with someone when they ask you about yourself?

5. After reading this chapter, what is one thing you will put into practice or one thing you will change in your life?

6. How can we, as a group, help you do this?

REACHING ADVENTUREOUS MEN

By: Greg Nass

Imagine you just completed construction on a new home, and to celebrate, you threw a housewarming party. It would feel good, even thrilling, as family, friends and neighbors admired and complimented the new home that you put time and effort into building.

What if you built a hot rod - say a classic Mustang or an old Firebird? After busting your knuckles and spending so much time in the garage, you wouldn't want to leave that pretty girl parked in the garage for no one to enjoy. You would take it out and proceed to properly burn the tires off and see what she can do.

Letting her rip around the corners or launching her from a red light would be exhilarating. To hear the horses come alive as your foot presses on the gas pedal would be an experience like no other and would surely get the blood flowing. Smelling the burnt rubber and looking in the rear view mirror at all the cars you just smoked makes you feel alive - it's thrilling to say the least!

So how do we show off our dream home or hot rod?

Do we sit at home on our big comfy couches, with plates of hors d'oeuvres and glasses of iced tea, hoping somebody will stop by?

Do we sit in the driver's seat of our hot rod, revving the engine and imagining that we are burning the tires off while parked in the garage?

I seriously hope not. In the same way, do we sit in the church building and wait for people to show up?

We must take the thrill to them. We must take church to them!

Jesus' very last words here on earth, the words that the Almighty knew would make the greatest impression, can be boiled down to one command - GO.

> *Jesus said, "All authority in heaven and on earth has been given to me. Therefore go and make disciples of all nations, baptizing them in the name of the Father and of the Son and of the Holy Spirit, and teaching them to obey everything I have commanded you. And surely I am with you always, to the very end of the age."* (Matthew 28:18-22, NIV)

In my opinion, this is the third greatest commandment in the Bible. The first is to love God with all our heart, and the second is to love our neighbor. If we are commanded to love God, love our neighbor, and GO, then why do we often sit idle?

Why don't we go to the people and invite them into our home more often?

Why don't we take the hot rod out for a trip around the neighborhood and tell someone how Jesus has impacted our lives?

I was once asked where I experience Christ the most.

My answer was quick - I feel closest to Him after climbing up a gnarly mountain trail on my mountain bike, as my heart pounds through my chest and the sweat rolls down my face searing my eyes.

Other times, I may be standing in the stream fly fishing when I hear His voice clearly speak to me.

Maybe it's while I am cutting the grass or simply driving my car.

The common denominator is that it's whenever I am free from the distractions of life's stresses - work, politics, bills, etc. For me, my mind is most clear when I am focused on simple tasks such as making small circles with my feet on my bicycle or putting bait in the stream.

Now I challenge you to close your eyes and ponder this simple question.

Where are you most distracted from life's complications?

Your answer will define where you can become the closest to God.

Write your answer here:

_____

During times of conflict, decision, or the unknown, go to this special place and ask God for direction. I am certain that He will answer you there.

Many men, especially those who lean towards the adventurous side, don't like sitting in buildings, chairs, pews, or even stadiums unless it's to see their favorite rock band, sports team, or motocross racers do extreme stunts. I know this first hand, because this is me. As much as I love church, worshipping God inside four walls can be a challenge as my spirit wanders elsewhere.

When men come together outside of church, they build strong relationships with each other that will better their chances to accomplish shared goals (summit a mountain, complete a race, finish a challenge that is outside of their comfort zones). By accomplishing these goals together, guys learn, firsthand, that nothing is too hard for God and there are no boundaries to what they can do.

David Morrow wrote one of my favorite books, "Why Men Hate Going to Church." This is a book that has confirmed a lot of the things that I have learned on my own over the years of doing men's ministry. There are a tremendous amount of good ideas within the book for risk taking ministry that will challenge men to step up and step outside to meet the Great Commission.

According to Morrow, "*Churches need men because men are natural risk takers—and they bring that orientation into the church. Congregations that do not take risks atrophy. Jesus made it clear that risk taking is necessary to please God. In the parable of the talents, the master praises two servants who risked their assets and produced more, but he curses the servant who played it safe. He who avoids all risk is, in the words of Jesus, 'wicked and lazy.'*"[1]

If we do not get up and out of our seats and go to the men, then we risk wasting the gifts and opportunities that God has given us.

One thing I've observed is that there are men who are uncomfortable in conferences or church services. Their guards may be up because society and the media have taught them that Christians are crazy, judgmental, and only want their money. They just don't know the truth.

Some men really struggle to sit inside and listen to people talk at you about things. They are like the kids sitting in class gazing out the window daydreaming about adventure. I have to be honest, over the years, I've been guilty.

Understanding their perspective, I believe that if we want to truly reach men, we need to give them opportunities to get outside where there is adventure, thrill, change, and some risk. Get grown men outside and away from the daily distractions of life, and they become alive. Get them doing the stuff they love to do, and everything changes. Now they become open and willing to listen. You are not speaking at them, but speaking with them. You've gained their trust through a common interest.

As they become comfortable in this environment, they are more open to hearing the truth about Jesus and His plan for their lives.

How do we get started? How do we reach this particular group of adventurous men?

1. GATHER UP A GROUP OF LIKE-MINDED ADVENTUROUS GUYS

How do we know who these guys are?

They are the dudes showing up to church in jacked up trucks or even Subaru outbacks. They have funny tan lines from being outside. They're often found standing in the back of the church. They miss Sunday services when it's nice outside. They wear Cabela's, North Face, or Columbia gear. They wear pants and shorts with multiple pockets and usually carry a pocket knife of some sort. Start looking for these characteristics and you will be able to quickly find your team.

Q: Name two men who fit the above description.

A1: _____

2. CREATE A CHALLENGE AND KEEP IT FUN AND ENJOYABLE.

Guys are born competitors and love a good challenge. This nature seems to go away as we get older. I can tell you that as I get older, I have less of a desire to race and more of a desire to watch people who do...maybe this just gives me a reason to ring my cowbell. Regardless, I still want to be challenged.

I still want the thrill of competition - wind blowing through my hair and dirt in my teeth. At the very least, I still want to watch people be challenged. Take men trap shooting, fishing, hiking, or biking. I've had great success with chili cook-offs as well. Whatever your team decides to do, turn it into a challenge with some sort of reward or at least "bragging rights." A small, humorous trinket goes a long way in these situations.

Q: What type of challenge speaks to you?

A2: _____

3. BE RESPECTFUL OF MEN'S TIME

Don't take up every Saturday morning or afternoon. Try Friday nights. Weeknights are also typically more accessible to guys since their families are busy with school and work.

Q: What day and time works best for you?

A3: _____

4. DON'T EMULATE A SUNDAY CHURCH SERVICE

Whatever you do, do not emulate a church service outside. Now don't get me wrong. I'm not saying to NOT have church outside. What I'm saying is don't do what they do inside, outside. Mix it up, keep it real, and don't start with a song, then an offering, a message, and finally an altar call. You must do something entirely different to reach adventurous men.

Hike a trail, and when you climb to the top of the mountain and reach the peak, then have church. Break down into study...or carry a guitar all the way up there and sing some manly hymns or songs.

Discuss some Scripture over a pan of sizzling bacon.

Read the Bible standing in the stream while you're wearing your waders getting ready to fish.

Meet on the mountain during hunting season for prayer and discussion at lunch time.

Don't over-plan on these events. When you get a group of Christian guys together, there is never an issue of finding something spiritual to talk about. If you have some guys who aren't Christian, well, that's a bonus and now you're on your way to meeting the Great Commission.

Q: Where would you like to worship God?

A4: _____

5. DON'T KEEP IT YOUNG

I believe there is an adventurous seed in each one of us, no matter how old or young we are or how domesticated we see ourselves.

I have always struggled with church groups that congregate based on age since at times I was considered too old to hang with the young adults at church. Instead of grouping by age, I suggest that we group by interests or other common factors.

I know guys who are in their 70's who can ride a mountain bike further, faster, and better than I can. So why would I want to exclude these guys from a Saturday morning bike ride for 20-30 year olds?

It seems strange when you think about us grouping people by age since that seventy-year-old might have just accepted Christ and will have a lot of questions that a twenty-year-old veteran in their faith can answer, or vice versa. We should group together based on common interests.

Q: Who are the oldest and youngest active guys in your church?

A5: _____

6. TRY SOMETHING NEW

Success can be achieved through failure. Yep, that's right. It's one of my favorite "me quotes."

As we try something and learn what doesn't work, we get to try something different until we finally succeed. Don't be afraid to try something new, but if it doesn't work, look at why and do something different.

Please don't keep doing the same thing and expect different results. Take notes at events, ask for feedback, send a survey out via email or have the guys complete a paper survey at the end of the event. This will help you learn what they want and don't want. There are a lot of ministry ideas that can be found at www.adventuremen.org.

Q: How can your church reach the adventurous community?

A6: _____

7. SERVANT EVANGELISM

When you finally have a group of guys who have built real relationships with each other and within their community of interest, it's time to start serving, or being the Good News.

Granted, it's tough to get guys to street witness, myself included. But anyone, and I mean anyone, can give someone a cold bottle of water on a hot summer day. Anyone can give someone a hot cup of coffee on a cold winter morning during hunting season. Anyone can give someone an energy bar at a race or outdoor endurance event.

Most importantly, anyone can say, "I just wanted to show you the kindness of Jesus Christ." When you say that sentence, or something similar, you are no longer just another nice guy promoting an organization. You have now given all the glory to God.

A book that I read early in my ministry walk is, "Conspiracy of Kindness" by Steve Sjogren. This book changed the way I witness to others and has opened the door for many candid conversations with strangers about Jesus Christ. This book was a game changer for me and laid out the servant evangelism approach that I just discussed.

According to Sjogren, "Servant Evangelism wins the heart before it confronts the mind. A small act of kindness nudges a person closer to God, often in a profound way as it bypasses one's mental defenses."[2]

Q: Where would you be most comfortable handing something out and how?

A7: _____

By going out of your church, you will actually be doing your church a favor. Yes, it's true. By stepping outside of the church, you will act as a recycling funnel and bring more people in. The most important part, though, is that it's not about your church or the numbers. It's all about bringing people to the Lord.

WHY?

Jesus went to the mountain when He wanted to be close to His Father. If He can do it, then why shouldn't we?

A CALL TO ACTION

Are you up for a good challenge? Are you ready for an amazing adventure with God outdoors doing what you love to do?

If you are, and I trust you are since you made it to the end of this book, then review your notes from this chapter and begin planning your first adventure event, designed to reach guys who typically don't go to the regular church service. Simply transfer everything that you wrote down previously to the following lines. This will be used as your launching plan.

Gather up your team:

(A1)_____

Create your first event:

(A2)_____

The day and time of your first event will be:

(A3)_____

Where and how will you make this a spiritual event :
(A4)_____

Two guys that you will invite first:

(A5)_____

Plan your second event:

(A6)_____

Plan your third event:

(A7)_____

Now that you have a clear plan of action, I want to leave you with this final thought, which is the third greatest commandment - GO.

BIG IDEA:

Jesus called us to GO. We need to get outside of the church walls to reach men. By challenging men and reaching them outside of the church, we will eventually bring them into our churches and to Christ. It all starts with reaching like-minded men outside of the church setting.

GROUP STUDY QUESTIONS:

1. Where are you most distracted from life's complications?

2. What type of challenge speaks to you?

3. What day and time works best for you to do men's ministry?

4. How can your church reach the adventurous community?

5. How does challenging men help reach them?

6. After reading this chapter, what is one thing you will put into practice or one thing you will change in your life?

7. How can we, as a group, help you do this?

BIBLIOGRAPHY

Chapter 1

1. Lewis Carroll, *Alice Adventure's in Wonderland,* (New York: Macmillan Company, 1898).

2. "Bryant Conant." BrainyQuote.com, accessed January 12, 2017, https://www.brainyquote.com/quotes/quotes/j/jamesbryan171089.html.

3. "Vince Lombardi." BrainyQuote.com, accessed January 12, 2017, https://www.brainyquote.com/quotes/quotes/v/vincelomba122285.html.

Chapter 4

1. "How to Detect Sinkholes: homeguides.sfgate.com/detect-sinkholes-43600.html

Chapter 6
1. James Strong. *Strong's Expanded Exhaustive Concordance of the Bible* (Nashville: Thomas Nelson, 2009).

2. Mike Ashcraft and Rachel Olsen, *My One Word* (Grand Rapids: Zondervan, 2012).

3. Kent R. Hughes, *Disciples of a Godly Man* (Wheaton: Crossway Books, 1991), 80.

Chapter 9

1. Abraham Joshua Heschel, *The Sabbath.* (New York: Farrar, Straus and Giroux, 1951), 16.

2. Abraham Joshua Heschel, *The Sabbath.* (New York: Farrar, Straus and Giroux, 1951), 21.

3. Abraham Joshua Heschel, *The Sabbath.* (New York: Farrar, Straus and Giroux, 1951), 21.

4. Wayne Muller, *Sabbath: Finding Rest, Renewal, and Delight in Our Busy Lives.* (New York: Bantam, 2013), 6.

5. Banning Liebscher, *Rooted: The Hidden Places Where God Develops You.* (Colorado Springs, CO: WaterBrook, 2016.), 35.

6. Richard A. Swenson. *The Overload Syndrome: Learning to Live within Your Limits.* (Colorado Springs, CO: NavPress, 1998)

Chapter 12

1. Richard Foster, *Celebration of Discipline: The Path to Spiritual Growth.* (New York, NY, Harper San Francisco, October 1, 1998), 127.

2. Richard Foster, *Celebration of Discipline: The Path to Spiritual Growth.* (New York, NY, HarperSanFrancisco, October 1, 1998), 132.

Chapter 13

1. "Disciple." Merriam-Webster.com. Merriam-Webster, n.d. Web. 12 Jan. 2017.

2. James Strong. *Strong's Expanded Exhaustive Concordance of the Bible.* (Nashville: Thomas Nelson, 2009)

Chapter 15

1. Rick Warren, *The Expanded Purpose Driven Life.* (Grand Rapids, Zondervan, 2002), 21.

Chapter 18

1. Andy Andrews, *The Traveler's Gift: Seven Decisions that Determine Personal Success.* (Nashville: Thomas Nelson, 2002), 85- 86.

Chapter 23

1. "Conviction." Dictionary.com., accessed January 10, 2017, http://www.dictionary.com/browse/conviction.

Chapter 26

1. Donald Gee, *The Fruit of the Spirit, Revised Edition, Faith Based— Pentecostal Classics.* (Springfield: Gospel Publishing House, 2012), Kindle Edition, 217-219.

2. Donald Gee, *The Fruit of the Spirit, Revised Edition, Faith Based— Pentecostal Classics.* (Springfield: Gospel Publishing House, 2012), Kindle Edition, 495-497.

Chapter 29

1. Charles Spurgeon, *She Was Not Hid..* http://www.spurgeongems.org/vols34-36/chs2019.pdf

2. Kevin Deyoung and Greg Gilbert, *What is the Mission of the Church?: Making Sense of Social Justice, Shalom, and the Great Commission.* (Wheaton, IL: Crossway, 2011), 46.

3. "Mathēteuō" #3100, *Hebrew-Greek Keyword Study Bible, ed. Spiros Zodhiates* (Chattanooga, TN: AMG Publishers, 2008), 3081.

4. Deyoung and Gilbert, *What is the Mission of the Church?: Making Sense of Social Justice, Shalom, and the Great Commission,* 46.

Chapter 30

1. Rebecca Manley. *Pippert, Out of the Saltshaker & Into the World: Evangelism as a Way of Life.* (Downers Grove: InterVarsity Press, 1979).

2. William Fay, *Share Jesus Without Fear.* (Nashville: Broadman & Holman Publishers, 1999), 12.

3. Mark Petterson, *"Strategic Conversations" in HIS Guide to Evangelism.* (Downers Grove: InterVarsity Press, 1977), 45.

4. Fay, *Share Jesus Without Fear*, pg 11.

5. Available at Amazon, Barnes & Noble, and www.initiateconversations.com

Chapter 31

1. David Morrow, *Why Men Hate Going to Church.* (Nashville: Thomas Nelson, 2011).

2. Steve Sjogren, *Conspiracy of Kindness.* (Minneapolis: Bethany House Publishing, 1993, 2003).

CONTRIBUTING AUTHORS:

BRIAN DONNACHIE is the Men's Ministry Director for the New Jersey District of the Assemblies of God. He has been the Senior Pastor at Living Hope Worship Center since 1999 and has also served in various ministry positions at churches throughout the greater Philadelphia area.

Brian and his wife Marianne live in Woodstown and have 3 daughters (Alyse, Amy, and Sara).

SHAWN BENTLEY is the Lead Pastor of Life Church of Hershey, a growing church located in the heart of Hershey, PA. Shawn also speaks at Creation Concert events and serves on the Board of Directors for 4One Ministries, the parent company of Mantour Ministries.

Shawn and his wife Kristal have been married since 1990 and have two sons, Kyle and Kory, and two daughter-in-laws, Haley and Nicole. Shawn is the proud grandpa to his first granddaughter, Audrey.

DAVID KENNARD has served at Riverside Community Church (RCC) in the Pittsburgh area for 17 years as the Adult Ministries Pastor. As RCC is a multi-site church, David is also the Site Pastor for their location at the Pittsburgh Mills.

David is married to Amie, and they have two children — Joshua and Jenna. David is a chocoholic, a tennis fanatic and loves electronic gadgets. He enjoys traveling, reading, biking and hanging out with his family.

TONY CRUZ received the call to ministry and began to preach at the age of sixteen.

Tony has spoken overseas and travels across the nation as the featured speaker at conferences, camps & conventions communicating with passion and conviction to adults and students . In addition to his travel, Tony and his wife, Elisha are lead pastors of a thriving church in Lewisburg, PA named Freedom Life Church. They have two boys and a little girl.

ROB STIEM is a devoted follower of Jesus Christ who is happily married for thirty-plus years to his beautiful bride, Margo. He's also the blessed dad of Erik (Kristen), Lindsay and Aaron. Rob and Margo are in their twenty-first year of pastoring the awesome folks at New Life Church in Grantville, PA.

Rob loves outdoor sports and activities. He's a lifelong avid Michigan Wolverines and Detroit Tigers fan.

SCOTT KRAMER serves as the Executive Pastor at Glad Tidings Church in West Lawn, PA. He is a teaching pastor and provides leadership to the adult ministry efforts of the church.

Scott loves to teach the Word of God, and has a passion for reaching this emerging generation. His hobbies include golf, church-league softball, competing in almost anything, and of course, spending time with his wife Kate and their two boys and little girl.

JOHN BOWMAN has lived in Dover most of his life. After graduating Dover High School in 1979, he entered the Navy until 1986 when he moved back to Dover with Andrea and their two sons, Paul and Sam. He worked as a printer until the Lord called him into ministry in 1995. John currently serves as Children's Pastor and Men's Ministry Director at Calvary Assembly of God in Dover, DE.

JAMES LEAKE is the Pastor Emeritus of Monroeville Assembly of God. He and his wife Becky just celebrated forty-four years of marriage. They enjoy working together, walking together, traveling together and serving the Lord together.

In 2005, James began to feel that God was calling him into another area of ministry. It was with much nostalgia that he resigned as pastor to enter into the field of part-time missions. He misses his friends at Monroeville Assembly, but he's excited about following God wherever He leads.

TOM REES has been the Penndel District Honorbound Director for the past 18 years. He has a passion for men's ministry and helping men achieve their potential as God's Sons. Tom also serves the Penndel District as the Director of US Missions and the Director of Church Development.

Tom is married to Sherry and they have two daughters, Courtney and Britney. He is an avid Eagles Fan and has a great sense of humor.

WAYNE SCHAFFER has been a pastor for 25 years and currently serves as the lead pastor of New Life Worship Center in Altoona, PA. Born into a pastor's home, Wayne gave his life to the Lord at the age of 5. At the age of 16, he was called into full time pastoral ministry while traveling with a Christian singing group.

He and his wife, Suzanne, have two children: son, Michael, and daughter, Carly. Pastor Wayne has a passion for "Kingdom Principles" to be lived out in the believer's life as well as through local churches working and serving their communities together. For more about Wayne's ministry visit: www.NewLifeAltoona.org.

WALTER G. SMITH is the husband of a phenomenal woman of faith named Lynn, the father of two adopted children, a grandfather as well as a great-grandfather. His family is the most cherished element of his life. Walt also greatly enjoys hunting, carving, oil painting, football and auto racing.

He has been a lead Pastor for forty years and has currently been the lead pastor of a terrific church in Altoona, PA for the past twelve years. Since 2010, he has served as the presbyter for the South Central West Section of the Assemblies of God in the Penn-Del Network encouraging ministers along with assisting churches in governance. Walt holds A/G credentials as a chaplain, ministering as a volunteer in the Federal Corrections Facility in Loretto, PA for over a decade.

JIM PENTZ is lead pastor of New Covenant Assembly and Presbyter of the North Central Section of the Penn-Del Ministry Network. He and his wife, Holly, have been married for forty-one years and have been blessed with two married daughters, their husbands, and four grandchildren.

DAVID TWISS has served as an Assemblies of God pastor for over three decades. He currently serves Green Ridge Assembly of God as Lead Pastor.

From March 2014 to the present, he serves as Presbyter of the Northeast Section of the Penn-Del Ministry Network. He is married to Laura, and they have a daughter, Melissa Timony; son-in-law, James Timony; daughter, Heather Cicilioni; son-in-law, John Cicilioni; son, Thomas Twiss, and granddaughter Lorelai Timony.

JAMIE HOLDEN is the founder of Mantour Ministries and the President of 4One Ministries. He is also an AG Associate Missionary with AG Missionary Church Planters and Developers, focusing on strengthening men and men's ministry.

Along with planning Mantour Conferences, Jamie enjoys writing and speaking to men. He's published three books, "Putting On

Manhood," "Legacy: Living A Life That Last," and "Get In The Game." He's a die-hard Denver Broncos fan who loves Rocky, the Elvis, and traveling with his sister, Adessa.

JAMIE ZIRKLE currently resides with his wife and son in his hometown of Winchester, VA. He is ordained with the Assemblies of God. Jamie continues to serve as a lay leader in Victory Church while he waits on God to open the next ministry opportunity for him. You can read more articles from Jamie at his blog (http:// jamiezirkle.wordpress.com/).

JOEY CULLEN, is originally from Boston, MA and currently serves as the Director of the Philadelphia Master's Commissions. Along with his wife Lori, Joey has a deep passion for young adults to be disciples and followers of Jesus. Together, they pour the theme "To know God and make Him known" into the lives of their students.

ANTHONY L. PELELLA grew up on Long Island in New York. He was a bodybuilding competitor and is training as a master's division boxer. He is an Assemblies of God minister in the New York district, and he has been senior pastor of Medford Assembly of God for more than two decades. He also serves as a Sectional Presbyter in the New York District.

He is the author of "The Bodybuilder." For more information or for guest speaking inquiries, visit www.thebodybuilderbook.com.

JOHN LANZA is the lead pastor at Glad Tidings A/G. Pastor John and Susan have been involved in church ministry for over 25 years, serving for 20 years as lead pastors of local A/G churches, and as the lead pastor at Glad Tidings Assemblies of God in Middletown, PA. He spent the majority of life in ministry in the Pennsylvania-Delaware district, but, most recently, he served as staff and then lead pastor in central Florida, planting a church in the Poinciana area.

John married his wife Susan while attending The University of Valley Forge. They are proud parents of three grown children: Megan, married to Andrew, Adam, and Meridyth; Pastor John and Susan are also the proud grandparents of Adalyn Rose, Isabel Grace, and Brenna Joy.

ROLAND COON serves as the Lead Pastor of Calvary Church where he has pastored for the past 39 years. He is also the Chairman of the Calvary Christian Academy School Board and the Presbyter of the Delaware Section of the Penn-Del Ministry Network. He also is on the Mantour Ministries/4One Ministries Board of Directors. He and his wife, Angela, have 3 children and 7 grandchildren.

JOHN KNUDSON is a husband, father and the pastor at LifeSpring Fellowship in Lititz, PA. John and his wife, Crystal, have been married for 18 years and have 7 children.

John was a youth pastor for 7 ½ years and then pastored a church in Potter County for 5 ½ years, before coming to Lititz in August 2016. John and Crystal are passionate about reaching people with the Gospel of Jesus Christ beyond the walls of the church whether that be in their community, state, nation, or world!

DAN COURTNEY has served as Lead Pastor for Crossroads Community Church in Mechanicsburg, PA since August 2010. Before coming to Christ and following Him in full-time ministry, Dan was the manager of a nightclub in Denver, Colorado. After a dramatic conversion experience on August 3, 1989, he dedicated his life to serving God in full-time ministry.

Dan and his wife Jen have two daughters. Dan is a former break dancer, an avid bowler, and a super-fan of the ~~San Diego~~ (Los Angeles) Chargers.

K.R. MELE became a believer and follower of Jesus Christ at the age of 21. That same year he was married and recently celebrated 28 years with his wife, Gina. They have two children, Luke and Olivia. Pastor K.R. served as a children's pastor in two churches before his family planted a new congregation, Family Life of Penns Valley in Centre Hall, in 2004. He enjoys spending time with his family, traveling with his wife, riding bikes, exercising, and finding creative ways to share Christ's love with others. You can learn more about Rock-n-Roll Ministries at: www.rocknrollministries.com.

WAYDE WILSON is a pastor, speaker, and the author of Circle of Swords, a book "for men who don't like to read books" based on the adventures of David's Mighty Men. Order your copy, or book Wayde for a Men's Event or a Fight for Your Family Weekend at: www.waydewilson.com.

CHAD STOECKER is the Lead Pastor at First Assembly of God in New Castle, PA. He has a passion to reach the family for Christ, and the best way in which to do so is to reach men.

Chad is most proud of the fact that he has been married to his college sweetheart, Michelle, for twenty years, and together they have raised three children to love Jesus with all of their hearts. When Chad's not watching the sports teams from his home state of Wisconsin (Packers, Brewers, Bucks & Badgers), you might find him playing a round of golf or reading any book/watching any movie about the Civil War.

BOBBY BASHAM is the Men's Director for the Potomac Section where he oversees Men's Ministries, Potomac Royal Rangers, Extreme Makeovers, and the Media Ministries for the District. He is also the Light for the Lost Director for the Northern region of the Potomac District. He has ministered overseas in several countries, led numerous construction projects, and has preached throughout the Potomac and Appalachian district.

Bobby lives outside of Winchester, Virginia with his wife, Gina, of over 28 years and their four sons. He enjoys the outdoors, sports, motorcycle riding and most of all, seeing God change lives.

STAN WILLIAMS was born into a pastor's home, received Christ at the early age of five, and received a call into the ministry as a pre-teen. He attended Northeast Bible Institute in Green Lane, Pa where he met his wife, Sheryll Emery. They have been married for 48 years and have three children and eight grand children. He is happy to say, all of his children are committed to following Jesus and are actively involved in ministry.

Stan served in pastoral ministry for 43 years, transitioning three years ago into a ministry that God has laid on his heart called "Boomerang" which focuses on his generation. He also serves as interim pastor having served three congregations in the last three years presently serving at Emmanuel AG in Allentown, PA.

TOM SEMBER and his wife Carolyn have been married for over 25 years and are blessed with three daughters: Jessica, Katherine, and Rebecca.

He is a 20 year veteran of the Buffalo Fire Dept. serving as a Lieutenant until an accident with the siren took close to 75% of his hearing. He has also worked in the construction industry, building houses and sole proprietor in the handyman service industry.

Upon his disability from the Fire Service, Tom went back to school and became a volunteer minister with the NY District of the Assemblies of God. He has pastored in NY and served as the NYDAG Men's Director for the state of NY.

JASON TOURVILLE is a husband, father, pastor, athlete, and author. He currently leads a thriving church, Shrewsbury Assembly since January 2013, and has been a full-time minister with the Assemblies of God since graduation from Valley Forge Christian College in 1995.

He now lives in Southern York County, PA with his wife Rene with their four kids (two boys and two girls) and a dog. What free-time is found, he likes spending with his family, and watching the kids in their interests. His weekly thoughts can be read at his blog www.JasonTourville.com.

TERRY DROST is the lead Pastor at Peckville Assembly of God. He, along with his wife Becky, grew up in Peckville Assembly of God Church. Terry loves northeastern Pennsylvania. He has a sincere desire to reach his community and beyond the valley!

Along with being a pastor and gifted speaker, Terry is an amazing and anointed worship leader. He and Becky have three children, Tyler, Dylan and Kyle. They are also very excited to have just welcomed their first granddaughter, Gracyn, into the world.

LEE ROGERS is a Youth Alive Missionary in Pennsylvania and Delaware. He is passionate about empowering students to share Jesus at school and equipping leaders to do the same. He is the author of "Initiate: Powerful Conversations that Lead to Jesus," and the lead author of "GOD SO LOVED: a student's guide to sharing Jesus at school." He is a graduate of the University of Valley Forge and a Doctoral candidate at Regent University. Lee resides in Central Pennsylvania with his wife Christine and his son Judah.

GREG NASS is the Founder of AdventureMen---a ministry launched in 2009 with the mission to help men experience Christ through adventure. Their largest annual event, AdventureFest, draws many men hungry for renewal, salvation, and outdoor adventure.

Greg is also an HonorBound Representative for the Assemblies of God PennDel District and is employed by the U.S. Government where he works on cyber security projects.

Greg lives in Bethel Park, PA with his wife Shannon, who is also a credentialed pastor with the Assemblies of God, their 12-year-old twin daughters, Naomi and Charlotte, and their beagle, Lucy.

PURCHASE A BOOK FOR A PRISONER

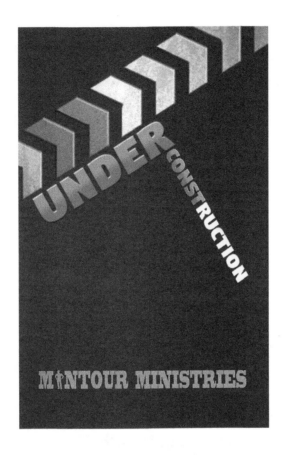

If you enjoyed this book, why not buy a copy
for a man in prison. You can help us reach more
men behind bars by donating at
mantourministries.com.

Mantour Ministries donates copies of our
curriculum to state and federal prisons.
We are reaching men behind bars with the gospel!

ALSO FOR MEN

It's time to get off the bench!

No matter where you came from, what you have done, or what you struggle with, God can use you! He can restore you. He can put you into the starting lineup and use you to change the world. Let's stop believing the enemy's lies.

Join us as we review the game tapes of biblical examples to learn what plays they made, where they fumbled, and how we can gain the victory. It's time to get in the game!

INCLUDES WORKBOOK AND GROUP STUDY QUESTIONS FOR SMALL GROUP MINISTRY

ALSO FOR MEN

How will you be remembered?

All men want one thing in life—to be remembered. Will you leave behind a good legacy or a bad legacy?

By reading the stories of godly men from the Bible, working through the study questions, and taking up the legacy challenges at the end of each chapter, you'll be well on your way to living a life that lasts.

Includes bonus workbook for use with small groups.

ALSO FOR MEN

IT'S TIME TO PUT ON MANHOOD

With 1 Corinthians 13:11 as a foundation, Putting On Manhood shows how to put childish ways behind you and become the man God designed you to be. With the help of God's Word, the Holy Spirit, and a band of brothers, you can grow into true, godly manhood.

INCLUDES GROUP STUDY QUESTIONS AND A WORKBOOK FOR SMALL GROUP STUDY